300 Sermon Outlines from the Old Testament

300
SERMON OUTLINES
from the
OLD
TESTAMENT

William H. Smitty

BROADMAN PRESS
Nashville, Tennessee

4222-42
ISBN: 0-8054-2242-0

Dewey Decimal Classification: 221
Subject headings: BIBLE. O.T.—SERMONS—OUTLINES, SYLLABI, ETC.
Library of Congress Catalog Card Number: 81-67996
Printed in the United States of America

Preface

Over a span of more than twenty-four years in the ministry I have often felt the need to preach on a particular subject but found it very difficult to develop my thoughts to that end. After much prayer and research, however, I have been startled more than a few times at finding just a simple statement surrounding a passage of Scripture which opened up a clear train of thought, resulting in a God-sent message for the hour. It is my prayer that these easy sermon builders will help many to find a pattern for developing those difficult but needed sermons which God would have them to preach. Many of them are from sermons which I have preached and some have simply been developed from my personal study and devotions. May God use them to accomplish his will through his willing servants.

WILLIAM H. SMITTY

Contents

GENESIS

The Creation *(Gen. 1:1-3)*
I. All Created Things Began in God (v. 1).
II. All Created Things Depend Upon God for Fruition (v. 2).
III. All Created Things Depend Upon God for Light (v. 3).
    A. Was so of original creation
    B. Is so of new creation (2 Cor. 5:17; John 1:4-5)

The Supreme Creation *(Gen. 1:26-27)*
I. Man Supreme Creation Because Created in Image of God
II. Man Supreme Creation Because Given Supremacy Over Other Created Things
III. Supremacy Included Equality (Male and Female)

In the Image of Three Divine Personalities *(Gen. 1:26)*
I. In the Image of God the Father
    A. Our Creator
    B. Our likeness to him
        1. Triune personality (body, soul, spirit)
        2. Intelligence
        3. Immortality, etc.
II. In the Image of God the Son
    A. Our Savior
    B. Our perfect example, etc.
III. In the Image of God the Holy Spirit
    A. Our Advocate, etc.
    B. Our source of power for every need

Shaped by the Master Potter *(Gen. 2:7)*
 I. The Form (clay in the potter's hands)
 II. The Life (life began upon a sacred foundation)
 III. The Soul (man's completeness began in the spiritual realm)

Sin's Curse and Man's Deliverance *(Gen. 3:1-24)*
 I. Sin's Curse
   A. Sin separated man from God (vv. 7-8).
   B. Sin made man afraid of God (vv. 9-10).
   C. Sin degraded man to a low estate (vv. 23-24).
   D. Sin enslaved man (vv. 17-18).
   E. Sin condemned man to death (v. 19).
 II. Man's Deliverance (v. 21, see also 1 John 1:7)
   A. The blood reconciles man to God (Eph. 2:13).
   B. The blood destroys fear of God's wrath (Rom. 5:8-9).
   C. The blood restores to man his right standing with God (Rom. 8:17).
   D. The blood delivers man from sin's slavery (Col. 1:13-14).
   E. The blood brings new life to the dead (Heb. 9:14).

Three Great Sins *(Gen. 3:6, compare 1 John 2:15-17)*
 I. The Lust of the Flesh
 II. The Lust of the Eyes
 III. The Pride of Life

Sin Equals Fear *(Gen. 3:8)*
 I. Man's Original Courageousness in God Implied
 II. Man False Enlightenment Becomes Darkness (vv. 5,7)
 III. Man's Enslavement to Fear

10

God's Call to Sinners *(Gen. 3:9-11)*
I. God Seeks the Sinner First (v. 9).
II. The Sinner Seeks to Hide from God (v. 10).
III. God Demands a Personal Accounting of the Sinner (v. 11).

A Savior Promised *(Gen. 3:15)*
I. The Conflict of Personalities
   A. Satan the tempter
   B. Mankind's fall
II. The Conflict of Seeds
   A. Satan's war against Christ
      ("shall bruise his heel")
   B. Christ's ultimate victory
      ("Shall bruise [his] head")
III. The Present Application
   A. Man is a sinner held under Satan's power.
   B. Christ broke Satan's power over mankind on the cross.

From Dust to Dust *(Gen. 3:19)*
I. Dust—Man's Origin
   A. But he became something more beautiful.
      ("God . . . breathed into his nostrils the breath of life; and man became a living soul," Gen. 2:7.)
   B. Then he became something very ugly (Gen. 2:16-17; 3:6).
II. Dust—Man's Doom
   A. Speaks of physical body
   B. Spiritual doom far more reaching and terrible
III. Christ—Man's Hope
   A. Second Adam (1 Cor. 15:21-22,45)
   B. New creation (2 Cor. 5:17)

Retrospect (*"And the Lord said unto Cain, Where is Abel thy brother?" Gen. 4:9*).
   I. Sin Cannot Be Overlooked.
      A. Because conscience is pricked by the retrospection of evil deeds
      B. Because God demands an accounting
   II. Sin Brings Out the Worst in Man.
      A. Cain murdered his brother and then denied it.
      B. The "Cain" in mankind would have us deny sin's presence
   III. Sin Must Be Reflected Upon and Dealt with Properly.
      A. Retrospection without repentance spells misery in the present life.
      B. Retrospection without repentance spells misery in eternity.

The Representative Walk (*Gen. 5:22-24; Heb. 11:9*)
   I. Enoch Is Representative of a Good Father.
   II. Enoch Is Representative of Genuine Christianity.
   III. Enoch Is Representative of the Rapture of the Church.

The Godward Walk (*Gen. 5:24*) (*"And Enoch walked with God . . .)*
   I. The Godward Walk Results in Fellowship with God.
   II. The Godward Walk Results in Service to God.
   III. The Godward Walk Results in Holy Living.
   IV. The Godward Walk Results in Assurance.
   V. The Godward Walk Results in Great Reward ("*. . . and God took him" Gen. 5:24*).

True Grace *(Gen. 6:8)*
I. Who Says Grace Is a New Testament Doctrine Only?
II. Who Will Question the Judgment of God Upon Those Not Under His Grace? (v. 13).
III. Who Will Deny That the Grace of God Is Unmerited? (Gen. 7:7).
IV. Who Can Say That God's Grace Is Not Sufficient? (Gen. 7:23).

The Wisdom of Obeying God *(Gen. 7:1)*
I. If Noah Had Disobeyed God's Command, Three Things Would Have Happened.
A. He and his family would have perished with the world outside.
B. The human race would have come to a complete and total halt.
C. The only righteous people upon earth would have made a mockery of God's grace.
II. The Wisdom of Noah's Choice
A. He knew that the ark was the only way of salvation for himself and his family.
B. He knew that the ark was capable of delivering them.
C. He knew that there was no salvation for those who were shut outside.

Noah's Altar *("And Noah builded an altar unto the Lord," Gen. 8:20.)*
Noah is remembered for his ark; he should also be remembered for his altar. The very first thing he did upon leaving the ark was to build an altar unto the Lord.
I. It Was an Altar of Worship.
A. Worship through thanksgiving
B. Worship through devotion (put God first)
C. Worship through service (did something for God)

II. It Was an Altar of Sacrifice.
   A. Offered self first (consecration)
   B. Offered the best he had (clean animals)
III. It Was an Altar of Separation (separated from the old world unto God).
   Application—What have you given to God since departing the old life of sin?

Progressive Scriptural Program of Worship *("And Noah builded an altar unto the Lord," Gen. 8:20.)*

  I. Altar—Stone
 II. Tabernacle—a Tent
III. Temple—a Building
IV. The Church—Combination of All the Above
   A. Christ the stone—church's foundation (Eph. 2:19-20; 1 Cor. 3:11)
   B. Our bodies the temporary tabernacle (2 Cor. 5:1; 1 Cor. 3:16; 6:19)
   C. Collectively we are the temple building (Eph. 2:21-22)

Babel *(Gen. 11:9)*

  I. Babel Represents Confusion.
   A. A confused people who forgot God
   B. Sinners are slaves to confusion
 II. Babel Represents the Judgment of God upon Sinners.
   A. All were judged (confounded).
   B. Individuals were judged (each one experienced a language barrier).
III. Babel Represents the Need of a Savior.
   A. The Babelites were totally depraved.
   B. Note their futile efforts at self-attained salvation (v. 4).

Abraham's Call *(Gen. 12:1-3)*

    Introduction—He was called Abram, but later Abraham. ("And I will . . . make thy name great," v. 2.)

I. The Importance of His Call (v. 1)
    A. It called for great sacrifice.
    B. It called for total commitment.
    C. It called for a new course in life.

II. The Imperative Involved in His Call
    A. A great covenant was involved.
    B. A great promise was involved.
    C. A great purpose was involved.
        1. Ultimate salvation of Israel
        2. Ultimate salvation of Gentiles

    Application—One man's obedience changed the course of history.

To Pitch or Not to Pitch *("And Lot . . . pitched his tent toward Sodom,"* Gen. 13:12.)

I. Lot's Move Was a Great Error (v. 13).
    A. It constituted yielding to sin.
    B. It proved to be a step in the wrong direction from which there was no turning back (the pull of sin) ("And Lot sat in the gate of Sodom," Gen. 19:1.).

II. Lot's Move Proved to Be Very Costly.
    A. It cost him his wife (Gen. 19:26).
    B. It cost him part of his family (Gen. 19:14).
    C. It cost him his dignity (Gen. 19:30-38).

For Personal Observation *("Thou God, seest me"* Gen. 16:13.)

I. If You Are Lost—How Soul-Searching!
II. If You Are Saved—How Comforting!
III. If You Are Backslidden—How Helpful!
    A. God seeks to check your sin.

B. God reminds you of his presence and concern.

C. God warns you of his disapproval and judgment.

A Divine Contract *(Gen. 17:1-3)*

I. God Clearly Stated His Position
("I am the Almighty God," v. 1a.).

II. God Clearly Stated His Requirement
("Walk before me," v. 1b.).

III. God Clearly Stated His Promise
("And I will make my covenant between me and thee,"
v. 2.).

IV. Abraham Clearly Understood His Part in the Contract
("And Abram fell on his face: and God talked with him,"
v. 3.).

Pillows of Stone *(Gen. 28:10-17)*

I. Jacob Made His Bed and Lay on It.

A. Deception toward his brother

B. Now on the run

C. No soft out for him

II. It Took God's Power to Make Stone Pillows a Blessing.

A. A great dream

B. A great promise

Application—If you are laying on pillows of stone commit
all to God and let him turn it into a blessing.

In God's Care *(Gen. 39:2)*

I. Joseph Had His Troubles.

A. Deceived by his brothers (Gen. 37:24)

B. A slave in Egypt (Gen. 39:1)

C. Tempted by his master's wife (Gen. 39:7)

D. Cast into prison (Gen. 39:20)

II. Joseph Was in God's Care.

A. Saved from death by a brother (Gen. 37:20-22)

B. Honored by his Egyptian master (Gen. 39:3-4)
C. Overcame temptation (Gen. 39:8-10)
D. God blessed Joseph in prison and delivered him from prison with great honor (Gen. 39:21; 41:39-40)

True Repentance *(Gen. 42:21)*
I. Recognition (guilt)
("we are verily guilty")
II. Remembering (conscience)
("we saw the anguish of his soul")
III. Reasoning (logic)
("therefore is this distress come upon us," see also Isa. 1:18)

EXODUS

God's Interest in One Life *(Ex. 2:2-11)*
  I. God's Timing—Baby Born (v. 2)
  II. God's Protection—Baby Hidden (v. 3)
  III. God's Providence—Baby Found (v. 6)
  IV. God's Care—Baby Nursed (v. 9)
  V. God's Guidance—Baby Grown (v. 11)
  VI. God's Plan—Man Called (Ex. 3:10)
  What great things came from that cradled babe!

"I AM THAT I AM" *(Ex. 3:14)*
  I. I AM All That Israel Needs
    A. They need deliverance from their hard taskmasters (I AM able to deliver them from their affliction, 3:7).
    B. They need deliverance from Egyptian bondage (I AM able to deliver them from Pharaoh's hand, 3:8).
    C. They need a leader to give them direction (I AM able to give them a deliverer, 3:10).
  II. I AM All That You (Moses) Need
    A. You need help (I AM able to provide strength for the task, 3:12).
    B. You need power (I AM able to stretch out my hand to provide the power against the king's rebellion, 3:19-20).
    C. You need a spokesman (I AM able to provide him, 4:14-16).
  Application—God is all we need in all circumstances.

A Worthy Contribution *(Ex. 4:2, "What is that in thine hand?")*

I. Some Examples
   A. We can't all be a Moses with his rod.
   B. We can't all be a David with his sling.
   C. We can't all be the lad with his small lunch.
   D. We can't all be the widow with her two mites.
   E. Our contribution may never measure up to the results of these.

II. Set a Precedent
   A. Start where you are with what you have.
   B. Don't worry about being as important as someone else.
   C. Don't try to make headlines.
   D. Don't try to duplicate Bible miracles.
   E. Simply contribute your best, regardless of how large or small, and God will be pleased.

Decisions of a Foolish King *(Ex. 5:2)*

I. Pharaoh's Foolish Question
   A. His ignorance
      ("Who is [God]?")
   B. His independence
      ("that I should obey his voice?")
   C. He learned the hard way

II. Pharaoh's Foolish Statement
   A. His irritation
      ("I know not the Lord")
   B. His irresponsibility
      ("neither will I let Israel go")
   C. But he did

The Judgment of Blood *(Ex. 12:12-13)*

I. The Judgment Announced (v. 12)
   A. The surety of the judgment

("I will pass through the land . . . and smite all the
firstborn . . . I will execute judgment")
B. The extent of the judgment
("both man and beast; and against all the gods of
Egypt")
II. The Judgment Averted by Blood (v. 13)
A. The blood covering
("And the blood shall be to you for a token upon the
houses where you are")
B. The blood covenant
("And when I see the blood, I will pass over you")
III. Judgment of Blood Because the Innocent Was Slain
A. The lamb's blood was the judgment paid in its death
for those who obeyed God's command.
B. Jesus became the Lamb of God for sinners (John 1:29).
1. The believer's sin has actually been judged in
Christ's blood.
2. The judgment of blood is only applicable for indi-
viduals who appropriate it by faith.

Victory *(Ex. 12:30-33)*

I. The Enlightenment (v. 30)
(Enemies awakened by God's judgment)
II. The Encouragment (vv. 31-32)
(God's people receive justice)
III. The Estrangement (v. 33)
(Release from retention)

Bickering Saints *(Ex. 14:10-11)*

I. The Grounds of Their Complaints
A. The visible dangers
1. Enemies closing in from behind
2. A raging sea before them
3. Towering mountains on the two sides
B. The halting confusion

20

1. They couldn't go back—the enemy was there.
2. They couldn't turn aside—the mountains were there.
3. They refused to go forward—the sea was there.
II. The Foolishness of Their Attitude
   A. God had brought them safely through other extremities.
   B. They bickered in the face of their greatest opportunity to see the rewards of faith (vv. 13-14).
   C. They could expect deliverance purely upon the basis of God's mercy and grace (vv. 21-22).
   D. Their foolish rebellion evoked a command from God leading to their salvation (v. 15).

Moving Forward *(Ex. 14:15)*
   I. Move Forward with Assurance of Victory Over Past Circumstances (v. 13).
   II. Move Forward with Complete Faith in God (v. 14).
   III. Move Forward with God's Ordained Man—your pastor— (v. 16).
   IV. Move Forward to a New Life—Opportunities for Service (vv. 30-31).

Get Going *(Ex. 14:15)*
   I. Stop Relying on the Past.
   II. Start Obeying Immediately.
   III. Strive for the Victory Ahead.

Manna and Mannerisms *(Ex. 16:15)*
   I. Grumbling (Selfishness, vv. 2,12)
   II. Fumbling (Greed, v. 20)
   III. Stumbling (Disobedience, vv. 27-28)

God's Supreme No-No *(Ex. 20:2-5)*

I. No Other Gods (v. 3)
  A. "I am the Lord thy God" (only one—v. 2)
  B. "I the Lord thy God am a jealous God"
     (demands sole adoration—v. 5)
II. No Graven Images (v. 4)
  A. Idolatry forbidden
  B. Any likeness of anything made for bowing to in
     worship constitutes idolatry
III. Give Examples—Modern Parallels of Breaking This Com-
     mandment

Sabbath Commandment for the Church *(Ex. 20:8)*

I. Keeping Our Terminology Straight
  A. Sabbath—Jewish
  B. Sunday—Christian
II. Remembering That a Sanctified Day Meant for All
  A. A new day dawned in Christ's resurrection
    1. Sabbath commandment not obsolete
    2. Obedience transferred to "Lord's Day"
  B. Keep it holy
    1. Law fulfilled in grace
    2. Liberty of grace not to diminish responsibility of
       worship
  C. Some reasons for obedience
    1. Love for God
    2. Love for Christian fellowship
    3. Love for scriptural instruction

Parental Honor *(Ex. 20:12)*

Introduction
  1. The Commandment says that we are to honor our parents.
  2. God is our heavenly parent (Father) and also deserves our
     special honor.

3. Make this comparison with this commandment and consider these three things.
  I. Reason: God's Command
  II. Requirement: Obedience
  III. Reward: God's Promise

Choosing a Side *(Ex. 32:26)*
  I. Are You Just for Your Side? (Selfishness)
  II. Are You All for Man's Side? (Flesh)
  III. Are You on God's Side? (Spiritual)

It's Your Choice *("Who is on the Lord's side?" Ex. 32:26)*
  I. The Moral or the Immoral?
  II. Kingdom of God or Kingdom of Evil?
  III. Winning Side or the Losing Side?

Consecrate Yourselves *(Ex. 32:29)*
  I. Consecrate Yourselves for the Assurance of Courage (Ps. 27:14).
  II. Consecrate Yourselves for the Assurance of Strength (Isa. 40:31).
  III. Consecrate Yourselves for the Assurance of Companionship (John 14:16).
  IV. Consecrate Yourselves for the Assurance of Joy (John 15:11).
  V. Consecrate Yourselves for the Assurance of Liberty (2 Cor. 3:17).

The Threefold Aspect of Consecration *(Ex. 32:29)*

I. Consecration as a Command ("Consecrate yourselves")

II. Consecration and Immediateness ("Consecrate yourselves today")

III. Consecration and Reward ("That he may bestow upon you a blessing")

LEVITICUS

Divine Blood *(Lev. 17:11)*
  I. Divine Origin
     A. Man was a lifeless form when first made
     B. God gave life to that lifeless form—gave it blood
 II. Defiled by Sin
     A. We are all blood relations to Adam (Acts 17:16)
     B. This relation connects us by sinner's blood (Rom. 5:17)
III. Divine Transfusion
     A. The Blood of Jesus Christ—("The blood of Jesus Christ his Son cleanseth us from all sin," 1 John 1:7.)
     B. Why?—Sinless sacrifice—("Behold the Lamb of God, which taketh away the sin of the world," John 1:29.)
     The Life Is In the Blood.

A Call to Complete Separation *(Lev. 18:1-5)*
  I. Complete Severing with Past Evil—("After the doings of the land of Egypt, wherein ye dwelt, shall ye not do," v. 3*a*.)
 II. Complete Abstinence from Evil Through New Temptations—("And after the doings of the land of Canaan, whither I bring you, shall ye not do," v. 3*b*.)
III. Complete Separation from Wrong Directions—("Neither shall ye walk in their ordinances," v. 3*c*.)
 IV. Complete Provision for a Separated Life (vv. 4-5)

NUMBERS

The Beauty of God's Blessing *(Num. 24:24-26)*
I. It Keeps (v. 24).
II. It Is Generous (v. 25).
III. It Gives Peace (v. 26).

The Saving Look *(Num. 21:4-9)*
I. The Selfish Look (vv. 4-5)
   A. It bred discouragement (v. 4).
   B. It bred a complaining spirit (v. 5).
   C. It bred rebellion against God (v. 5).
   D. It bred rebellion against God's anointed (v. 5).
II. The Inward Look (vv. 6-7)
   A. It came through judgment (v. 6).
   B. It produced an awareness of sin (v. 7).
   C. It brought an awareness of a needed remedy (v. 7).
III. The Upward Look (vv. 7b-9)
   A. Going to God in prayer (v. 7b)
   B. Hearing God's instruction
   C. Heeding God's instruction
   D. The saving look of faith (John 3:14-15)

The Sure Consequence of Sin *(Num. 32:23)*
Introduction—There are some things about sin of which we can be certain.
I. It Is Certain That Sin Is a Reality.
   A. Being so, it cannot escape the eyes of God.
   B. Being so, peace cannot come to the guilty.
II. It Is Certain That Sin Will Be Punished.
   A. Often revealed and dealt with in the present life

B. Unforgiven sin will be revealed and dealt with in eternity

III. It Is Certainly Foolish to Sin and Try to Get By.
   A. God demands repentance.
   B. Self-judgment and repentance place our guilt upon Christ.
   C. Refusal on our part brings the wrath of God.

DEUTERONOMY

Obedience *(Deut. 5:32-33)*
  I. The Threefold Command
    A. To observe God's Word (v. 32*a*)
    B. To stay on the straight and narrow (v. 32*b*)
    C. To walk in God (v. 33*a*)
  II. The Threefold Promise (v. 33)
    A. Life—"that ye may live"
    B. Well-being—"that it may be well with you"
    C. Protection—"that ye may prolong your days in the land"

Preparation for Death *("And the Lord said unto Moses, Behold, thy days approach that thou must die," Deut. 31:14.)*
  I. The Application
    A. Godly men have no fear of death.
    B. Death is sure and godly men are prepared when God summons (1 Thess. 5:9).
  II. The Contrast
    A. Ungodly men fear death.
    B. Judgment is sure and ungodly men will be there when God summons (Heb. 9:27).

The Sure Foundation *("Underneath are the everlasting arms," Deut. 33:27.)*
  I. Arms Denote Personality
    A. Personal Creator (Gen. 1:1; 2:7)
    B. Personal Provider (Ps. 23:1)
    C. Personal Foundation (1 Cor. 3:11)
  II. Arms Denote Support

    A. Redemption (Eph. 1:7)
    B. Refuge (1 John 2:1)
    C. Reassurance (Heb. 4:15)
III. Some Armless Foundations
    A. Atheism (Ps. 14:1)
    B. Skepticism (John 8:43-45)
    C. Materialism (Matt. 6:19-20,33)

JOSHUA

A Time to Arise *(Josh. 1:2)*

I. When a New Leader Arises
   A. A time must come for departing from past leadership.
   B. Beware of "Preacher Religion."
   C. Arise and follow God's man of the hour.
II. When New Challenges Arise
   A. Putting past accomplishments and failures to rest
   B. Reaching out for present and future blessings and accomplishments
III. When New Opportunities Arise
   A. "Now"—there is a time which may be the only right time.
   B. "Go over"—being at the right place at the right time can mean the difference between success and failure.

The Word *(Josh. 1:8)*

I. Word Not to Be Forsaken
   ("shall not depart out of thy mouth")
II. Word Not to Be Left Unstudied
   ("thou shalt meditate therein day and night")
III. Word Not to Be Left Unheeded
   ("observe to do according to all that is written therein")
IV. Faithfulness to the Word Not Left Unrewarded
   A. "Thou shalt make thy way prosperous."
   B. "Thou shalt have good success."

Wet Feet, Dry Ground *(Josh. 3:7-17)*

I. Hearing God's Messenger (v. 7)
   A. Message based on God's Word

30

B. Messenger Approved of God
II. Obedience Calls for Faith
   A. Dangers of overflowing river
   B. God said "wade in"
III. Miracle of Dry Ground
   A. God put his priests and the ark of the covenant out front to prove his power.
   B. People passed over on dry ground.
   C. God's power awaited beyond the trial.

Choose You (*"Choose you this day whom ye will serve,"* Josh. 24:13-15.)
  I. This Is a Personal Appeal to You (you have to make a choice).
  II. This Is a Paramount Appeal to You (importance of your choice).
  III. This Is a Pressing Appeal to You (immediateness of your choice).

The Urgency of a Right Choice (*Josh. 24:15*)
  I. Persons Are Needed in God's Service ("Choose you.")
  II. Persons Will Serve Some Thing, Cause, or Master ("Choose you . . . whom ye will serve.")
  III. Persons Will Let Neither the Choice nor the Service Admit of Any Delay ("Choose you this day whom ye will serve.")
  Application—Your devotion lies somewhere at this very moment. Is it with God?

JUDGES

Sin and Repayment *(Judg. 1:1-7)*
Introduction
1. One cannot mete out injustice upon others and get by.
2. Adoni-bezek is a classic example of this truth.
3. His example teaches three things.
   I. Justice Will Come to the Unjust.
      A. The justice of God can be hard.
      B. The justice of God is always fair.
   II. Justice May Be Delayed for a Season.
      A. One may go through life with an attitude of winning through inhuman cruelty.
      B. In time God's hour of judgment will come.
   III. Repentance Can Come Too Late.
      A. Adoni-bezek was sorry only after he was captured.
      B. Justice was sure and deadly.

Cooperation and Victory *(Judg. 7:21)*
   I. Plan
      A. It was conceived in the mind of God
      B. Necessity of scriptural foundation
   II. Man
      A. Each man was appointed a place in the plan
      B. Necessity of unity in God's work
   III. Stand
      A. The encampment was large, the soldiers few
      B. Necessity of complete dependence upon God

Steps to Spiritual Ruin *(Judg. 16)*

I. Enticement ("Entice him," v. 5)

II. Indolence (Sleeping)—("And she made him sleep upon her knees," v. 19.)

III. Unawareness ("And he wist not that the Lord was departed from him," v. 20.)

IV. Captivity (v. 21)
- A. Confining—"Philistines took him"
- B. Blinding—"And put out his eyes"
- C. Binding—"Bound him with fetters of brass"
- D. Grinding—"He did grind in the prison house"

The Backslider's Bereavement *(Judg. 16:20-21)*

I. The Awakening

II. The Forsaking

III. The Overtaking

Spiritual Digression *(Judg. 16:20-21)*

I. Strength from God

II. Severance from God

III. Silence of God

IV. Servitude to the World

RUTH

Devotion and Reward *(Ruth 1—4)*
  I. She Followed with Devotion (1:16-17).
  II. She Gleaned with Devotion (2:3).
  III. She Was Rewarded for Her Devotion (4:13).
  IV. Her Devotion Resulted in a Great Heritage (4:17).

Contrast of Decisions *(Ruth 1:14-18)*
  I. Orpah's Decision (vv. 14-15)
    A. A kiss without loyalty
    B. A departure unto false gods
  II. Ruth's Decision (vv. 15b-18)
    A. Loyalty to Naomi
    B. Loyalty to God
  III. The Patterns Before Us
    A. The indifference of Orpah
    B. The felicity of Ruth
    C. The decision is yours

1 SAMUEL

Spiritual Sickness and God's Remedy *(1 Sam. 7:1-17)*
  I. Israel Was a Sick Nation (vv. 1-2).
  II. Israel Was Offered Only One Remedy (v. 3).
  III. Israel Applied God's Remedy (vv. 4-8).
  IV. Israel Received Healing from God Through Obedience (vv. 9-17).

The Sin of Saul *(1 Sam. 15)*
  I. Its Nature
     (He disobeyed God for selfish reasons.)
  II. Its Scope
     (It affected the entire nation of Israel.)
  III. Its Outcome
     (It brought the curse of his dethronement as king of Israel.)

Faith's Glorious Triumph *(1 Sam. 17:45-47)*
  "For the battle is the Lord's" (v. 47*b*).
  I. Faith Blots Out Fear (v. 45*a*).
  II. Faith Relies Upon Fact (v. 45*b*).
  III. Faith Claims Victory Over Seeming Unsurmountable Circumstances (v. 46).
  IV. Faith Pledges All Glory to God (v. 47).

Rewards of a Little Man *(1 Sam. 17:4-11,20-27,32-37,48-58; 18:1-5)*
  I. God Rewarded Him with Victory Over the Giant.
  II. He Was Rewarded with the Respect of His Nation.
  III. He Was Rewarded with the Friendship of a Prince.
  IV. He Was Rewarded with Honor and Promotion by a King.

2 SAMUEL

The Reward of Mephibosheth *(2 Sam. 9:7)*
 I. It Was Unmerited.
   A. "For Jonathan thy father's sake"
   B. So of Christians (for Christ's sake)
 II. It Brought Great Blessings.
   A. An inheritance
   B. Provision for every need
   C. Compare with Christian's blessings

No Place Like Home *(2 Sam. 23:15)*
  I. Natural Man's Heart Craves a Domestic Home.
 II. Spiritual Man's Heart Craves a Church Home.
III. Holy Man's Heart Craves a Heavenly Home.

1 KINGS

A Great Man's Downfall *(1 Kings 11:9-12)*
I. Solomon, a Man of God-Given Wisdom
II. Solomon, a Man Taken by His Carnal Nature
III. Solomon, a Man Given to Disobedience
IV. Solomon, a Man Given a Second Chance Based Upon Repentance

"Let It Rain, Let It Pour" *(1 Kings 18:41-46)*
I. Elijah's Faith
   A. His vision wasn't just for rain, but for abundance of rain (v. 41).
   B. His vision was followed by a prayer of faith (v. 42).
II. Elijah's Faith Tested
   A. First look revealed nothing (v. 43)
   B. His faith endured seven other looks (vv. 43*b*-44*a*) (a little cloud)
III. Elijah's Faith Rewarded
   A. Faith to forewarn Ahab (v. 44*b*)
   B. God let it pour (v. 45)
   C. God protected Elijah (v. 46)

The Caveman *(1 Kings 19:9)*
I. Three Things Elijah Sought in the Cave
   A. Concealment from his enemies
   B. Ease from godly labor
   C. Escape from reality
II. Three Things the Cave Actually Became to Elijah
   A. A cave of humiliation
   B. A cave of cowardice
   C. A cave of despair

2 KINGS

Seeking and Finding God's Power *(2 Kings 2:1-15)*
I. Elisha Recognized the Source of God's Power (vv. 1-8)
II. Elisha Requested God's Power (v. 9)
III. Elisha Received Specific Instructions on Attaining God's Power (v. 10)
IV. Elisha Was Rewarded with God's Power (vv. 11-14)
V. Elisha Revealed God's Power to Men (v. 15)

Wrong Attitudes About Deliverance *(2 Kings 5:1-14)*
I. Thinking Money Can Buy It (v. 5)
II. Thinking Man's Instructions Will Give the Answer (v. 6)
III. Thinking the Power of It Lies Within the Hands of Man (v. 7)
IV. Thinking It Comes Through Sensationalism (v. 11)
V. Thinking God's Plan for It Can Be Altered (v. 12)

God's Grace *(2 Kings 5:1-16)*
I. Sent Through Human Agency
   A. The "Little Maid" (vv. 2-3)
   B. Naaman's Servants (v. 4)
   C. Kings of Syria and Israel (vv. 5-8)
   D. Elisha the Prophet (v. 8)
II. Often Questioned
   A. Elisha's instructions (v. 10)
   B. Naaman's attitude (vv. 11,12)
   C. A sensible deduction (v. 13)
III. Obedience Required (v. 14)
   A. The dipping (faith)
   B. The cleansing (followed obedience)
   C. The gratitude expressed (v. 15)

The Outsider *(2 Kings 5:1-17)*

(A Syrian captain—an outsider to Israel—an outsider to God)

I. Description of the Outsider (v. 1)
II. Directions for the Outsider (vv. 2-5)
III. Deliverance of the Outsider (vv. 8-14)
IV. Delight of the Outsider (v. 15)
V. Dauntless Decision of the Outsider (v. 17)

The Sin of Self-Will *(2 Kings 5:11-13)*

Here we have the lesson of a man who almost lost his only opportunity for God's grace because of the sin of self-will.

I. His Rebellion (self demanded healing his way)
II. His Pride (self said "there is a better way")
III. His Turning Away (self would have kept him enslaved to his sickness)

Application—Naaman was able to overcome self-will in time to prevent total destruction (vv. 13-14).

1 CHRONICLES

Consecration, Why? *(1 Chron. 29:5)*
   I. Because a Request from God Is Really a Command
  II. Because an Unconsecrated Heart Is an Unhappy Heart
 III. Because the Anointing of God for Service Depends upon
        Consecration
  IV. Because a Lost World Depends Upon Our Consecrated
        Service

Characteristics of Good Servants *(1 Chron. 29:5)*
   I. Willingness
       "Who then offereth willingly"
  II. Industrious
       "This day"
 III. Consecrated
       "To consecrate"
  IV. Self-giving
       "Himself"

2 CHRONICLES

If *(2 Chron. 7:14)*
    (The "I" in the *if* is the key to revival)
  I. Importance of Humility and the Christian Individual
  II. Importance of Prayer and the Christian Individual
  III. Importance of Repentance and the Christian Individual

The "I Wills" of God Concerning Revival *(2 Chron. 7:14)*
    Introduction—When God's people meet God's conditions
    for revival, he makes three great promises.
  I. "I Will Hear."
  II. "I . . . Will Forgive."
  III. "I . . . Will Heal."

What Is Revival? *(2 Chron. 7:14)*
  I. Primarily Revival Is not Evangelism
  II. Primarily Revival Is not Emotionalism
  III. Primarily Revival Is Emulation
    A. To excel in obedience to God's formula
    B. To imitate the life of Christ

A Threefold Prayer for Saints in Need *(2 Chron. 14:11)*
  I. "Our God"
    A. The only sure source of help
    B. The greatest foundation upon which to lay our needs
  II. "Help Us"
    A. It is our privilege to seek help from God.
    B. It is our duty to show our trust in God by seeking his
        help.

III. "For We [Trust in] Thee"
   A. The reason why we can seek God's help
   B. The reason why we can know he will sustain us in our
      hour of need

National Misery *(2 Chron. 15:3-4)*

(Three specific things which lead to national misery)
   I. Forsaking God ("A long season . . . without . . . God")
   II. Forsaking the Bible (religious education) ("Without a
       teaching priest")
   III. Forsaking Law (law and order)—("Without Law")

Three Hindrances to Tranquility *(2 Chron. 15:3-5)*

("There was no peace," 5a)
   I. Lack of God's Presence ("Without the true God," v. 3*a*)
   II. Lack of Christian Education ("Without a teaching priest,"
       v. 3*b*)
   III. Lack of Respect for Law—Without Law (v. 3*c*)

God's Work in Man's Behalf *(2 Chron. 16:9)*

   I. He Looks Upon Us
      ("The eyes of the Lord")
   II. He Acts in Our Behalf
       ("Run to and fro")
   III. He Has Personal Interest in All His People
        ("Throughout the whole earth")
   IV. He Is the Personal Defender of His People
       ("Shew himself strong in the behalf of them")
   V. He Has a Condition
      ("Whose heart is perfect toward him")

Seven Lamps We Must Keep Lit *(2 Chron. 29:1-9)*

Introduction—The priests of Israel were charged with dressing the lamps in the tabernacle so that they would never go out (v. 7).

I. The Lamp of God's Word
II. The Lamp of Fundamental Doctrine
III. The Lamp of Genuine Worship
IV. The Lamp of the Christian Witness
V. The Lamp of Christian Morality
VI. The Lamp of Christian Home Life
VII. The Lamp of Immortality

Application—Extinguish these lamps and the human race has no hope

Yielded Lives *(2 Chron. 30:6-9)*

(Some examples of lives yielded unconditionally)

I. Look What Noah Did with an Ark
II. Look What Moses Did with a Rod
III. Look What David Did with a Sling
IV. Look What Isaiah Did with a Vision
V. Look What Jesus Did with a Cross

Early Surrender to God *(2 Chron. 34:1-7)*

I. A Young Heart Is Susceptible to God.
II. A Young Heart Dedicated to God's Will Has Limitless Possibilities.
III. A Young Heart Following God's Law Will Be Safe from the Snares of His Surrounding Society.

EZRA

A Time for National Repentance *(Ezra 9:5-15)*
(Text: vv. 5-6)
   I. National Repentance Can Grow Only from National Shame.
  II. National Repentance Can Start Only from Deep Personal Sorrow in the Spiritual Realm.
 III. National Repentance Can Be Evoked Only When God's People Separate Themselves from the Abominations of Sinners.

God Forbid *(Ezra 9:12)*
    I. That His People Be Unequally Yoked with Unbelievers in Marriage
   II. That His People Seek Peace in the Worldliness of the World
  III. That His People Seek Satisfaction in the Wealth of the World
   IV. That His People, Through Disobedience, Spoil a Godly Heritage for Their Children

NEHEMIAH

The Power of Positive Purpose (*"For the people had a mind to work," Neh. 4:6b)*

I. The Miracle
   A. Consider what was accomplished out of seeming useless material.
   B. Consider what was accomplished out of seeming unsurmountable circumstances.
   C. Consider what was accomplished in spite of problems with labor force.
II. The Method
   A. Unity of effort
   B. Vision of accomplishment
   C. Overcoming barriers through good leadership
III. The Mind
   A. Guided by divine will
   B. Marshaled by common intelligent output
   C. Realization of success by use of resources at hand

God's Business First *(Neh. 6:1-4)*
   ("I am doing a great work, . . . I cannot come down," (v. 3.)
   I. God's Business Is Too Important to Cease for the Sake of Appeasing the Enemy.
   II. God's Business Is Too Important to Leave Off When There Is Knowledge That Doing So Will Lead to "Mischief."
   III. God's Business Is Too Important to Forsake, Though Many Attempts Be Made to Detract Us from It.

The World's Attitude Toward God's Work *(Neh. 6:15-16)*
   I. At Times They Can't Deny the Effects of God's Work, Though They Would Like To (vv. 15-16c)
  II. At Times They Can't Close Their Ears to God's Work, Though They Would Like To (v. 16a)
 III. At Times They Can't Hide Their Shame in Contrast to God's Work, Though They Would Like To

The Victory of Accomplishment *("So the wall was finished," Neh. 6:15a)*
   (Five things can be recounted from this story of triumphant success)
   I. Realizing the Need
  II. Rallying to the Cause
 III. Resisting Oppressive Forces
  IV. Relying Upon the Power of Prayer
   V. Rejoicing in Triumph

Faithfulness to God's House *(Neh. 10:39)*
   I. Faithfulness to the Tabernacle Expected
  II. Faithfulness to the Temple Expected
 III. Faithfulness to the Synagogue Expected
  IV. Faithfulness to the Church Expected (Heb. 10:25)

True Faithfulness *("And we will not forsake the house of our God," Neh. 10:39b)*
   I. This Was the Cry of a Delivered People
  II. This Should Be the Cry of Every Christian
 III. This Should Be a National Cry

A Declaration of Loyalty (*"And we will not forsake the house of our God," Neh. 10:39b.*)
- I. It Came Through Awareness of Past Failures in Respect to Such Loyalty.
- II. It Was Born Out of the Contrite and Broken Spirits of God's People.
- III. It Was Made Upon the Basis of Gratitude for the Privilege to Renew Such Loyalty.

ESTHER

God Chooses a Queen *(Esther 2:1-10; 4:14)*
  I. God Chose an Orphan Through Wise Mordecai.
  II. God Chose a Captive Jew Disguised Beyond Detection.
  III. God Chose a Beautiful Maiden to Captivate the King.
  IV. God Chose a Queen to Save His People.

God's Timing *(Esther 4:13-14)*
  I. God's Clock Is Never Wrong.
   A. There is always a definite time for responding to God's will.
   B. Men may forfeit such advantage to promote God's will.
  II. God's Message for the Hour Is Never Wrong.
   A. There is always a human voice to speak God's message for the hour.
   B. Individuals are personally responsible to either hear or reject God's message.
  III. God's Purpose for the Hour Cannot Be Frustrated.
   A. Men may attempt to do so and bring destruction both upon themselves and others.
   B. God's purpose will succeed, even if by an alternate route.

JOB

True Tranquility *(Job 1:1-22)*
  I. Job Was At Peace with God (v. 1).
  II. Job Was At Peace with the World (Richly Blessed, v. 3).
  III. Job Was At Peace with His Family (vv. 4-5).
  IV. Job Was At Peace from Satan's Power (vv. 6-10).
  V. Job Was At Peace in the Midst of Great Testing (vv. 11-22, esp. v. 22).

God's Testimony Concerning Job *(Job 1:8)*
  I. A Man of Perfection
     "There is none like him in the earth, a perfect . . . man."
  II. An Upright Man
     "An upright man"
  III. A God-fearing Man
     "One that feareth God"
  IV. A Man Who Hated Evil
     "And escheweth evil"
     Application—Though greatly tempted by Satan, as shown in verses 13-19, Job retained the high standards of God as revealed in verses 20-22

The Divine Hedge *(Job 1:10)*
  I. Satan Hates It (cannot penetrate it).
  II. God Provides It (blessing of his protection for the righteous).
  III. Man Dwells Within It (grace revealed toward the saints).

Great Questions in Job *(2:1-13)*

I. God's Question to Satan (vv. 2-3)
  A. God's testimony of Job's integrity (v. 3)
  B. Satan's challenge and God's response (vv. 4-6)
  C. The resultant attack upon Job (vv. 7-8)
II. The Question of a Nagging Wife (v. 9)
  A. The only thing Job had left was his life and a nagging wife.
  B. She challenged him to defy God.
III. The Question of a Man of Unshakable Integrity (v. 10)
  A. He rebuked his wife's evil suggestion.
  B. He challenged the right to expect the goodness of God without expecting some bad in life also.
  C. He refused to sin by speaking evil of God.

A Humbling Revelation *(Job 11:7-11)*

I. The Incomprehensible God
II. The Unlimitable God
III. The Vainness of Carnal Man's Attempt to Find Out God

The Great Transition *(Job 14:14; 19:15-16)*

I. A Great Question (14:14)
  A. "If a man die, shall he live again?"
  B. Physical death is sure
II. A Great Proclamation (14:14)
  A. "Till my change come"
  B. After death we await the resurrection of the body
III. A Great Transition (19:25-26)
  A. Our Redeemer shall come again.
  B. We shall stand with him in the latter days.

Where to Find God *(Job 23:3)*

    (There are three definite places where we find God.)

  I. We Find God in Our Innate Being (Ps. 14:1).

  II. We Find God in the Scriptures (Gen. 1:1).

  III. We Find God in Jesus Christ (John 1:1,14).

Death *(Job 30:23)*

    I. The Scriptural Affirmation

   II. The Personal Acceptance

  III. The Divine Appointment

       Conclusion—Compare Hebrews 9:27

PSALMS

The Worldly Man and the Godly Man—A Contrast
(Ps. 1:1)
I. Notice the Declining Status of the Ungodly Man
  A. In youth—"Walketh," but in the counsel of the ungodly
  B. In middle years—"Standeth," but in the way of sinners
  C. In old age—"Sitteth," but in the seat of the scornful
II. Notice the Increasing Status of the Godly Man
  A. In youth—"Walketh," but in the counsel of the godly
  B. In middle years—"Standeth," but with the righteous
  C. In old age—"Sitteth," but in the chair of wisdom (teaching, etc.)

Three Sins to Shun *(Ps. 1:1)*
I. The Ungodly's Counsel
   (To walk therein is dangerous)
II. The Sinner's Way
   (To stand therein is degrading)
III. The Scorner's Seat
   (To sit therein is destructive)

The God Blessed Man *(Ps. 1:1-3)*
I. Blessed Because of His Character in Relation to God (v. 1)
II. Blessed Because of His Integrity in Relation to God's Law (v. 2)
III. Blessed Because of His Overflowing Life in Relation to God's Righteousness (v. 3)

The Wickedness of the Wicked Shall Come to an End
(Ps. 7:9)
   I. It Can End in Conversion.
   II. It Can End in Death.
   III. It Can End in Hell.

God's Name *("How excellent is thy name," Ps. 8:1-9.)*
   I. Excellent Because of His Power (vv. 1-2)
   II. Excellent in Comparison to His Creation (vv. 3-4)
   III. Excellent Because of His Benefits to Mankind (vv. 5-9)

Man *(Ps. 8:3-4)*
   I. Introspection—"What is man?"
      A. It shows the weakness of man in comparison to his Creator.
      B. It shows the instability of man in comparison to the perfect order of God's universe.
      C. It shows the need of man for the divine touch in comparison to all else God has ordained.
   II. God-trospection—"Thou art mindful of him"
      A. God made man as a perfect being in the scheme of his perfect creation.
      B. God made a plan to return man to his originally ordained purpose in spite of his fall.
      C. God honored man through giving his Son to bring about his regeneration.

What Is Man? *(Ps. 8:4)*
   I. He Is a Unique Creation (Gen. 1:26-27).
   II. He Is a Sinner by Choice (Gen. 3:1-6).
   III. He Is of Special Concern to God (Gal. 4:4).
   IV. He Can Be Recreated in Spiritual Birth (John 3:3).

Foolish Pride *(Ps. 10:4)*
I. Self-righteous Pride Will Not Merit God's Mercy.
II. Educational Pride Will Not Alter God's Word.
III. Environmental Pride Will Not Produce Godward Happiness.
IV. Social Pride Will Not Win God's Favor.
V. God-Rejecting Pride Will Bring Eternal Doom.

A Goodly Heritage *(Ps. 16:6)*
I. How True When We Consider Our Great Freedom as Americans
II. How True When We Consider Our Religious Freedom
III. How True When We Consider Our Spiritual Freedom in Christ

Three Great Blessings *(Ps. 16:11)*
I. To Have Been Shown the Path of Life in Christ
II. To Live in God's Presence in Fullness of Joy
III. To Have the Hope of Future Pleasures Forevermore

Desires of the Spirit *(Ps. 19:7-14)*
("More are they to be desired than fine gold," v. 10)
I. What They Are
   A. The law of the Lord (v. 7)
   B. The testimony of the Lord (v. 7)
   C. The statutes of the Lord (v. 8)
   D. The commandments of the Lord (v. 8)
   E. The fear of the Lord (v. 9)
   F. The judgments of the Lord (v. 9)
II. The Results
   A. They warn (v. 11)
   B. They reward (v. 11)

C. They cleanse (v. 12)
D. They keep (v. 13)
E. They produce innocence (v. 13)
F. They call forth praise (v. 14)

The Pilgrim's Progress *(Ps. 23:4)*

I. There Are Valleys for All to Walk.
("Through the valley")
II. We Can't Always Walk in the Sunshine.
("Shadows")
III. We All Must Face Some Dangers.
("Death")
IV. We Can Have Victory in the Valleys.
("I will fear no evil")
   A. Assurance—"For thou art with me"
   B. Safety—"Thy rod and thy staff they comfort me"

God's Face *(Ps. 27:8)*

Here we have:
I. An Invitation to Dwell in God's Presence
II. An Opportunity to Delight in God's Character
III. An Obligation to Discover God's Will

Patience *("Wait on the Lord he shall strengthen thine heart," Ps. 27:14)*

I. Be Patient in Loneliness
("The Lord will take me up," v. 10).
II. Be Patient When Facing Enemies
("Teach me . . . O Lord . . . lead me" (v. 11).
III. Be Patient When God Seems Far Away (v. 12).
   A. He is nearer than you think (v. 13).
   B. He gives courage (v. 14).
   Conclusion—"Wait, I say, on the Lord" (v. 14).

Godward Confidence *(Ps. 31:14)*

I. Confidence and Trust Are Inseparable.
("I trusted in thee")
II. Confidence and Personal Application of God's Ability Are Inseparable.
("O Lord")
III. Confidence and Personal Commitment Are Inseparable.
("I said, Thou art my God")

Public Worship—Why? *(Ps. 34:3)*

I. Assembly for Public Worship Is God's Plan
II. Unity in Public Worship Pleases God
III. Magnitude in Public Worship Exalts God

Thy Tongue *(Ps. 34:13)*

I. Note the Personal Responsibility in Regard to Right Use ("Thy tongue")
II. Note God's Exhortation to Apply Self-Control Over It ("Keep . . . from evil")
III. Note the Results of Wrong Use of It ("Speaking guile")

The Excellency of God's Loving-Kindness *(Ps. 36:7-8)*

I. It Is Unmerited
("Under the shadow of thy wings")
II. It Is Based Upon Faith Alone
("Men put their trust")
III. It Offers Great Reward
A. Abundant satisfaction
B. Eternal pleasures

Seven Words of Good Advice for Believers *(Ps. 37:3-8)*.

I. Trust (v. 3)
II. Delight (v. 4)

III. Commit (v. 5)
IV. Rest (v. 7)
 V. Cease (v. 8)
VI. Forsake (v. 8)
VII. Fret Not (v. 8)

Delight and Desire *(Ps. 37:4)*
 I. A Promise ("He shall give thee the desires of thine heart.")
   A. This is God's promise to his saints.
   B. This is a scriptural promise.
   C. This is a promise to be claimed.
 II. The Prerequisite ("Delight thyself also in the Lord")
   A. Delight to serve God
   B. Delight to pray
   C. Delight to study God's Word

Seeking After God *(Ps. 42:1)*
 I. Three Things Which Cause Men to Seek After God
   A. His nature
   B. His conscience
   C. His need
 II. Three Ways in Which God Responds to the Man of Faith
   A. Gives him a new nature
   B. Cleanses his conscience
   C. Satisfies his needs

There Is a River *(Ps. 46:4)*
 I. The River of Christ's Blood (John 1:29)
 II. The Far-Reaching Effects of His Blood
   A. "Streams" from rivers go in many directions.

57

B. "Streams" from rivers carry life to outlying areas.
C. "Streams" suggest the many methods and means of spreading the gospel.
III. The Eternal Values Expressed
A. Salvation on earth
B. Rejoicing in eternity
  1. Soulward
  2. Godward

David's Seven Steps to Repentance *(Ps. 51)*

I. He Recognized His State of Misery (vv. 5,8,11-12,14)
II. He Recognized His Personal Guilt (v. 3).
III. He Recognized God's Justice in Judgment (v. 4).
IV. He Recognized His Personal Responsibility for Repentance (vv. 6,16-17).
V. He Recognized His Uselessness to God's Service Without Personal Repentance (vv. 12,13,15-16,18-19).
VI. He Recognized God's Mercy as the Only Grounds Upon Which to Repent and Seek Forgiveness (v. 1).
VII. He Recognized That Full Pardon and Thorough Cleansing Would Come with True Repentance (vv. 2,7,9-10).

Facts and Faith for Backsliders *(Ps. 51)*

I. David Committed Sin (v. 3*b*)
("My sin is ever before me")
II. David Did Not Try to Cover His Sin (v. 3*a*)
("I acknowledge my transgressions")
III. David Went to the Right Source to Confess His Sin (v. 1)
IV. David Craved the Joy of Renewed Fellowship with God (v. 12)
V. David Had Faith in God's Power to Forgive Him and to Cleanse His Heart (vv. 7-10)

Lost and Found (*"Restore unto me the joy of thy salvation,"*
Ps. 51:12.)
Note—It is not salvation which is lost, but rather the joy of
it. Notice three things stated in this relation:
I. The Joy of Salvation Comes from God.
("Thy salvation")
II. The Joy of Salvation Can Be Lost
("Restore . . . the joy")
III. The Joy of Salvation Can Be Found Again.
("Restore unto me the joy")

The Creed of Atheism (*Ps. 53:1*)
I. It Is the Fool's Creed.
("The fool hath said")
II. It Is a Deception of the Heart
("In his heart," see also Jer. 17:9)
III. It Is an Ignorant Philosophy.
("There is no God")
A. The scriptural proof
B. The visible proof
C. The innate proof

Supreme Fellowship (*Ps. 73:24-25*)
I. It Belongs to Those Who Follow God's Counsel.
("Thou shalt guide me with thy counsel")
II. It Assures Us of Great Reward.
("And afterward receive me to glory")
III. It Is a Far-Reaching Fellowship.
A. "Whom have I in heaven but thee?"
B. "There is none upon earth that I desire beside thee."

The Great Contrast *(Ps. 78:53)*
I. There Is a Wide Margin Between the Godly and the Ungodly.
   A. Between Israel and Egypt—The Red Sea
   B. Between the Christian and Sinner—Wrath of God
II. There Are Two Sides to a Margin and All Are on One Side or the Other.
   A. Those on God's side
      1. Led by him
      2. Kept safe in him
      3. Delivered from fear
   B. Those on the wrong side
      1. They are enemies of God.
      2. They are enemies of God's people.
      3. They are doomed to destruction.

Right Attitudes Toward Revival *(Ps. 85:1-7)*.
I. The Motive Must Be Right.
II. The Message Must Be Right.
III. The Method Must Be Right.
IV. The Meditation Must Be Right.

Three Facts Regarding Revival *(Ps. 85:6)*
I. The Urgency
   ("Revive us again")
II. The Agency
   ("Wilt thou")
III. The Expectancy
   ("That thy people may rejoice in thee")

Need of Revival *(Ps. 85:6)*
I. Ancient Israel Needed It.
   ("Wilt thou not revive us again?")

II. Our Nation Needs It.
("Wilt thou not revive us again?")
III. Modern Church Needs It.
("Wilt thou not revive us again?")
IV. Individual Christians Need It.
("Wilt thou not revive us again?")
V. Spiritual Renewing Depends Upon It.
("That thy people may rejoice in thee")

Adjectives of Eternal Bliss *("Glorious things are spoken of thee, O city of God," Ps. 87:3.)*
I. Joy (Ps. 16:11)
II. Beauty (1 Cor. 2:9)
III. Knowledge (1 Cor. 13:12)
IV. Perfection (Rev. 21:4)
V. Reunion (1 Cor. 13:12)

The Sure Dwelling Place *(Ps. 90:1-2)*
I. Based Upon Past Testimony (v. 1)
II. Assured By the Infinity of God (v. 2)
III. Appropriated By Confidence That God's Record Is True

Reasons for Giving Thanks *(Ps. 100)*
I. Because It Is the Call of God to All People (vv. 1-2)
II. Because of the Knowledge of God's Supremacy (v. 3)
III. Because Gratitude Is a Virtue God Expects of Us (v. 4)
IV. Because the Rewards of God Are Perpetual (v. 5)

A Christian's Song *("Unto thee, O Lord, will I sing," Ps. 101:1.)*
I. Christians Have Reason to Be the Happiest People in the World.

61

II. Christians Should Find It Easy to Sing Praises to God Concerning His Mercy.

III. Christians Ought to Sing Praises to God, Even in Judgment.

("For whom the Lord loveth he chasteneth," Heb. 12:6.)

God's Benefits and Our Obligations *(Ps. 103:2)*
I. We Should Claim Them.
II. They Should Call Forth Our Praise.
III. They Should Call Forth Our Service.

Praises for God's Provision *(Ps. 107:1-9)*
I. The Recognition (v. 1)
II. The Redemption (vv. 2-7)
III. The Renown (v. 8)
IV. The Reward (v. 9)

One Way *("And he led them forth by the right way," Ps. 107:7.)*
I. There Is Only One "Right" Way.
A. Jesus ("I am the way," John 14:6.)
B. Narrow way (Matt. 7:14)
II. The Wrong Way Is the Fool's Way.
A. Because enticed in world's way (Matt. 7:13)
B. Because it leads to destruction (Matt. 7:13)
III. God Would Lead All in the "Right" Way.
A. Must be willing to be led
B. Where he leads us to "a city of habitation"

Gleanings of Truth *(Ps. 119:1-8)*
("Thy Word is truth," John 17:17.)
I. The Blessing (vv. 1-2)

II. The Better Way (v. 3)

III. The Backward Look (v. 4)

IV. The Bright Hope (vv. 5-6)

V. The Bold Promise (vv. 7-8)

God's Word *(Ps. 119:145-160)*

I. It Is to Be Kept (vv. 145-146).

II. It Gives Hope (v. 147).

III. It Is to Be Meditated Upon (v. 148).

IV. It Is the Foundation of Truth (v. 151).

V. It Can Be Fully Trusted (v. 152).

VI. It Has Quickening Power (vv. 154,156).

VII. It Is to Be Loved (v. 159).

VIII. It Is Enduring (v. 160).

The Satisfying Effects of God's Word *(Ps. 119:169-175)*

I. It Gives Understanding (v. 169).

II. It Delivers (vv. 170,173,175).

III. Its Teaching Calls Forth Praise (v. 171).

IV. It Leads to Witnessing (v. 172).

V. It Delights (v. 174).

The Rewards of Witnessing *(Ps. 126:6)*

I. Requirements of Good Witnesses

A. Willing Service
   ("He that goeth forth")

B. Sincere Effort
   ("And weepeth")

C. Bearing truthful witness
   ("Bearing precious seed")

II. Rewards of Good Witnesses
  A—Victory over obstacles encountered—"Shall doubtless come again"
  B—Sincerity (weeping) repaid with joy—"With rejoicing"
  C—Fruition assured—"Bringing his sheaves with him"

The Great Contrasts *(Ps. 138:6)*
  I. The God Who Is High and Man Who Is Lowly
   A. The condescending God
     1. Because of his love for man
     2. Proved his love through Jesus Christ
   B. The humility required to have God's favor
     1. Mankind subject to the supremacy of God
     2. Mankind can in no way deserve God's favor
  II. The Humble and the Proud
   A. God's preference is shown to the humble.
   B. God knows the proud, but "afar off."

PROVERBS

God's Formula for a Happy, Successful Life *(Prov. 3:1-10)*

I. Perseverance and Peace
   A. Condition (v. 1)
   B. Results (v. 2)
II. Approval and Recognition
   A. Condition (v. 3)
   B. Results (v. 4)
III. God's Guidance
   A. Condition (vv. 5-6)
   B. Results (v. 7)
IV. Good Health
   A. Condition (v. 7)
   B. Results (v. 8)
V. Material Success
   A. Condition (v. 9)
   B. Results (v. 10)
   Application:
   1. In these verses it becomes obvious that God wants his people to live happy and successful lives.
   2. But it is also obvious that he intends for us to meet certain conditions in order to do so.

Consider God's Way *(Prov. 3:5-6)*

I. Consider This Directive as God's Plan
II. Consider This Directive as God's Will
III. Consider This Directive as God's Command
IV. Consider This Directive as God's Promise

Ungodly Pride *(Prov. 8:13)*

I. Pride Is Denounced as Sin.
II. Pride Increases in Its Domination of the Sinner.
III. Pride Is Designated as a Sin Hated of God.
IV. Pride Denies the Supremacy of God in One's Life.
V. Pride Drags the Soul Down to Destruction.

Witness of the Righteous *(Prov. 11:30)*

I. The Righteous Man Bears Fruit.
   A. It is his nature to produce fruit.
   B. He produces life-giving fruit.
II. The Wise Man Wins Souls.
   A. He does so by the means of heaven-sent wisdom.
   B. He does so by a wise use of methods.
   C. He does so by wise, tactful effort.

The Sevenfold Consequence of Ungodly Companionship

("A companion of fools shall be destroyed," Prov. 13:20.)

I. It Will Destroy Character.
II. It Will Destroy the True Vision of Sin's Reward.
III. It Will Destroy One's Sensitivity to Important Truths.
IV. It Will Destroy One's Ability to Gain the Best from Life.
V. It Will Destroy All Possible Vision of a Proper Example.
VI. It Will Destroy One's Ability to Cope with Life's Tragedies.
VII. It Will Destroy One's Ability to Face Death and Eternity.

The Right and Wrong of It *(Prov. 14:12)*

I. When Wrong Is Right (here we have the order of natural thinking)
   A. When man convinces himself that mere sincerity is the prerequisite to being in the right way

B. When personal sin is excused in favor of one's own religious philosophy

C. When one closes his mind to truth and chooses the way of error

II. When Right Is Wrong (here we have God's appraisal of the natural order in man's thinking)

A. When sincerity leads to deception

B. When self-knowledge leads to darkness

C. When self-righteousness leads to destruction

The All-Seeing Eyes *(Prov. 15:3)*

I. "Beholding the Evil"

A. This should strike terror in the hearts of sinners.

B. God keeps a record (Rev. 20:12).

C. God looks within (1 Sam. 16:7).

II. "And the Good"

A. This should encourage Christians to walk in holiness.

B. This should encourage commitment to service (Rom. 12:1-2).

C. This should be a source of comfort to the righteous.

D. This should inspire the saints with a sense of security.

God's Distance to the Wicked *(Prov. 15:29)*

I. God Does Not Wish It So (2 Pet. 3:9).

II. God Wishes to Close the Gap Between Himself and Sinners (Ps. 145:18-19).

III. God Will Not Close the Gap When Man Wishes to Keep It Open (Rom. 1:18-21).

A Senseless Supposition *(Prov. 17:16)*

(That any price can buy wisdom for willing fools)

I. Wisdom Is Within Reach of Fools.

II. Wisdom Has a Price.

III. Fools Have No Heart to Secure Wisdom.

Training New Christians *(Prov. 22:6)*

Introduction

1. We realize that the application of this verse is to the proper training of children.

2. However, this verse could also be applied to the proper training of young Christians who are babes in Christ.

I. The New Christian Is in Great Need of Proper Spiritual Training.

II. We Too Often Neglect the Young Christian After His (New) Birth as Though He Were Full Grown.

III. We Have Problem Christians in Their Advanced Stages Because They Did Not Receive Proper Training as "Babes in Christ."

Conclusion (Paraphrase) "Train up a new Christian in the way he should go; and when he is old he will not act like a child."

A Divine Warning *(Prov. 22:22-23)*

I. The Strong Taking Advantage of the Weak Has Been a Curse of the Ages.

II. A Benevolent Spirit Finds No Season for Oppression.

III. Poverty Proves the Unconcern of the Comfortable.

IV. Cruelty to the Unfortunate Will Bring Divine Retribution (v. 23).

Seven Reasons for Giving God the Heart *(Prov. 23:26)*

I. Because It Is God's Request

II. Because It Is God's Wish

III. Because It Is in God's Interest
IV. Because It Is in Our Interest
V. Because God Is Worthy
VI. Because God Holds Title to It
VII. Because It Is the Wisest Move We Can Ever Make

The Uncertain Tomorrow *(Prov. 27:1)*
I. Life's Ambitions Can End in Death.
II. Life's Attainments Can Be Lost in Bankruptcy.
III. Life's Activities Can End in Bad Health or a Mental Breakdown.
IV. Life's Attractions Can End in Sin and Eternal Damnation.
V. Life's Only Alternative to Uncertainty Is Found Through Saving Faith in Jesus Christ.

Boastful Sinners *(Prov. 27:1)*
I. They Boast of Future Plans with No Assurance of Life Beyond Today.
II. They Boast of Present Security in Material Things with No Salvation to Face Eternity.
III. They Ignore the Warning "Boast Not" and Refuse to Humble Themselves Before God.
IV. They Put Off Salvation Until Tomorrow, Knowing Not What Tomorrow May Bring Forth
Application—Have security now—let this day bring forth salvation for your soul (2 Cor. 6:2).

Stumbling Blocks *(Prov. 28:10)*
I. Beware of Holding Any Soul's Welfare in Bondage.
II. Beware of Abusing the Righteousness of Another.
III. Beware of Setting Snares for Young Believers.
IV. Beware of Any Part in the Downfall of God's Child.

Folly of Fools *(Prov. 28:26)*

I. The Folly of Trusting One's Own Heart
II. The Folly of Missing God's Wisdom
III. The Folly of Missing God's Deliverance
IV. The Folly of Walking the Road to Hell

A Renewed Vision *(Prov. 29:18)*

Christians need to help the world to have a vision of God like:

I. Isaiah (Isa. 6:1-3)
   A. Exalted (v. 1)
   B. Reverenced (v. 2)
   C. Glorified (v. 3)
II. David (Ps. 139:1-4)
   A. A searcher of hearts (v. 1)
   B. All knowing (vv. 2-4)
III. Elisha (2 Kings 2:14)
   (A God of power)
IV. John (Rev. 20:11-15)
   A. A God of judgment
   B. Point out that John's Gospel and Epistles speak much of God's love.
   C. However, John made it clear beyond doubt that one day God's grace will end for sinners.

A Verse in Reverse *(Prov. 29:18)*

I. "Perish"
   A. This is the most horrifying word in the Scriptures.
   B. This word is descriptive of the fate of all the unsaved.
   C. This word describes a condition to which there is no end.
II. "People"
   A. All people are at the center of God's concern.

B. All people have a right to hear the gospel.

C. All people who would escape God's wrath must do so through personal faith in Jesus Christ.

III. "Vision"

A. Vision is expected of all Christians.

B. Vision is the expectation many Christians avoid.

C. Vision is the answer to world evangelism if turned into action.

Hindrances to Proper Vision *(Prov. 29:18)*

I. Vision Does Not Come When There Is Poor Leadership.

II. Vision Does Not Come When Doubt Prevails.

III. Vision Does Not Come to an Unconcerned Heart.

IV. Vision Does Not Come to a Self-Satisfied Life.

V. Vision Does Not Come When God's Word Is Forgotten (v. 18*b*).

Christian Mothers *("Her children rise up, and call her blessed," Prov. 31:28.)*

Some Reasons:

I. Her Motherhood
(Gave them life)

II. Her Ministry
(Cares for them)

III. Her Methods
(Mature decisions for their proper growth)

ECCLESIASTES

What Is Life? *(Eccl. 1:2)*
I. Life Is Vanity Until It Finds Fulfillment in God.
II. Life Is Vanity Unless It Is Lived in Dedication to God.
III. Life Is Vanity Unless It Comes Down to the Grave in Unbroken Fellowship with God (see 12:13).

Condemned Religious Extremity *(Eccl. 7:16)*
This text warns against:
I. Extreme Fanaticism
II. Extreme Ceremonialism
III. Extreme Pharisaism
IV. Extreme Emotionalism
V. Extreme Self-Righteousness
VI. Extreme Philosophicalness

Death and Accounting *(Eccl. 8:8)*
Here we are awakened to three great truths:
I. The Powerlessness of Man to Prevent Death
II. The Battle Is Won or Lost According to Preparedness or Unpreparedness
III. The Wicked Will Give a Full Account of His Wickedness After Death

Man's Sin *(Eccl. 8:11)*
I. The Degree of Man's Sin Is an Abuse of God's Patience.
II. The Degree of God's Patience Often Holds Back His Immediate Judgment.
III. The Degree of Man's Depraved Condition Can Be Changed Only Through the New Birth.

Innate Wickedness *(Eccl. 8:11)*
I. The Long-suffering of God Is Expressed in Relation to Man's Wickedness.
II. Man Takes Advantage of God's Leniency and Feels Secure in Sinning.
III. The Natural Depravity of Man's Heart Is Completely Set to Do Evil.
IV. Man Is Powerless to Control His Depraved Nature Without Divine Help.

Man's Madness and Ending *(Eccl. 9:3)*
I. Man's Moral Insanity
II. Man's Irreligious Foolhardiness
III. Man's Unavoidable Rendezvous (Death)

Rendering Good Deeds *(Eccl. 9:10)*
I. Notice Two Things
   A. The urgency of work while alive and well
   B. The impossibility of work after death
II. Heed the Message
   A. All of our God-given faculties are committed to our control.
   B. God can use only that which we commit to his will.
III. Consider the Choice
   A. We can choose to make the well-being of others our first business.
   B. We can choose to live only unto ourselves and go down to the grave having failed God.
   Conclusion: "Do it with thy might"

Christian Responsibility *(Eccl. 9:10)*
I. Each Christian Has Duties to Be Performed in This Life.
II. Unfinished Responsibilities Cannot Be Attended to Beyond the Grave.
III. Death Does Not Excuse Us from the Consequence of Neglected Responsibilities.

A Life-Changing Command *(Eccl. 9:10)*
This command gives:
I. Purpose to Life
II. A Plan for Fruitful Living
III. Power for Successful Accomplishments
IV. Preparation for Peaceful Dying

The Sin of Ingratitude *(Eccl. 9:14-15)*
I. Great Problems Often Seem Unsurmountable.
II. The Answer to Great Needs Often Come from the Most Unlikely Source.
III. Our Gratitude Is Often Very Short-Lived.

Think Young *(Eccl. 12:1)*
Introduction
1. There are a lot of false ideas about old age floating around.
2. There is really no such thing as old age spiritually speaking.
3. In the eyes of God there are at least three ways in which a person never becomes too old:
I. A Person Never Grows Too Old to Become a Christian
   A. Age is no barrier to God's power to save.
   B. Even what little may be left of life is of value to God.

II. A Person Never Grows Old Enough to Retire from Service to God.
   A. The aged can have a great ministry through prayer.
   B. Many great soul-winners have been confined or handicapped in some way.
III. No One Ever Grows Too Old to Be Blessed of God.
   A. Age is no barrier to God's love.
   B. Fellowship with God at any age is a great source of blessing.
   C. Learning to be content with conditions in life and trusting God fully is the secret of true blessings.
   Conclusion—Think young in spirit

Modern Hindrances to the Young *(Eccl. 12:1)*
   I. Delinquent Parents
   II. Rapid Advances of a Scientific Age Which Questions God's Word
   III. The Temptations of an Adult World
   IV. A Lack of Being Loved
   V. Attitudes of Society Which Too Quickly Pushes Them into Adulthood
   Conclusion—Young people, look to God. ("Remember now thy Creator in the days of thy youth")

The Days of Youth *(Eccl. 11:9 to 12:1)*
   (Four reasons for giving God the days of your youth)
   I. Because of His Love for You
   A. He made you (Psa. 139:14).
   B. He made for you a way of salvation (2 Cor. 5:12).
   II. Because You Are Now Living in the Most Important Years of Your Life
   A. The impressionable, teachable years
   B. The time to prepare a whole life of service to God

III. Because You Are the Future Church
   A. Dedication now can preserve its spirit
   B. You will be responsible for what the church is tomorrow.
IV. Because Evil Days Are Coming
   A. They can influence you against worship.
   B. Give all your time, present, and future to God now.

A Challenge for the Young (*"Remember now thy Creator in the days of thy youth," Eccl. 12:1*).

   I. Abel Did.
      A. It cost him his life
      B. Better to die serving God than to live like a Cain
  II. Jacob Did.
      A. He made some terrible blunders
      B. Better to blunder trying to serve God than to become a weakling like Esau
 III. Joseph Did.
      A. It brought persecution upon him
      B. Better to be persecuted for a season than to go the way of sinning brothers
  IV. David Did.
      A. He had to fight the giant
      B. Better to stand on God's side in the battle than to trust in the strength of man
   V. The Young Lad Did.
      A. It cost him his lunch
      B. Better to give all to Christ and see faith work than to be doubters like the disciples

Fear of God *(Eccl. 12:13)*
   I. It Is the Mark of the Wise (Ps. 111:10).
  II. It Results in Obedience.
      ("Keep his commandments")
 III. It Prompts Us to Recognize Our "Whole Duty" to God.

SONG OF SOLOMON

Devotions of the Upright *("The upright love thee," Song of Sol. 1:4.)*
  I. Their Gratitude Expressed in Service
 II. Their Admiration Made Known Through Communion with Him
III. Their Love Expressed Through Complete Submission to His Will
 IV. Their Sincerity Expressed Through Holy Living

Springtime *(Song of Sol. 2:10-13)*
   Some lessons we need to be reminded of:
  I. The Flowers of Youth in the Church Must Be Properly Attended
 II. The Harvest of Souls Without the Church Must Be Properly Approached
III. The Rejoicing of God's People for Sustenance Through the Winter Must Be Properly Acclaimed

Beware the Little Foxes *(Song of Sol. 2:15)*
  I. Some Sit in the Church Pews to Spoil the Work.
 II. Some Plot in Church Classes to Spoil the Truth.
III. Some Stand in the Pulpit to Spoil the Salvation of Souls.
 IV. Some Gossip Outside the Church to Spoil Its Outreach.

ISAIAH

Affliction *(Isa. 1:5)*
  I. Affliction Is Unnecessary.
     ("Why should ye be stricken any more?")
 II. Affliction Is Invited by Rebellion Against God.
     ("Ye will revolt more and more.")
III. Affliction Is the Result of Unreasoning Minds.
     ("The whole head is sick," see v. 18.)
 IV. Affliction Brings Unbearable Stress.
     ("The whole heart [is] faint.")
     Application—Regeneration rather than affliction is clearly
     being offered here by God.

Invitation to Reason *(Isa. 1:18)*
  I. The Voice
     ("Come now, . . . saith the Lord.")
 II. The Verdict
     ("Your sins be as scarlet . . . they be red like crimsom.")
III. The Victory
     ("They shall be as white as snow, . . . they shall be as
        wool.")

God's Penalty for Rebellion *(Isa. 1:20)*
  I. Based Upon Refusing to Hear God's Plea
     ("Come now," v. 18)
 II. Based Upon the Rejection of God's Promise
     ("Though your sins be as scarlet, they shall be as white as
        snow," v. 18.)
III. Based Upon God's Own Testimony
     ("For the mouth of the Lord hath spoken it," v. 20.)

Humbled, Yielded, Commissioned *(Isa. 6:1-9)*
  I. Humbled (vv. 1-5)
     A. By the vision of God
     B. By the vision of self
 II. Yielded (v. 8)
     A. By hearing God's call
     B. By answering God's call
III. Commissioned (v. 9)
     A. To go
     B. To tell

Prince of Peace *(Isa. 9:6)*
  I. The Prince
     A. A child born to be adored
     B. The Son given to be worshiped
     C. The Prince crowned as King of kings
 II. The Peace
     A. Because he is our wonderful Savior
     B. Because he is our comforting Counselor
     C. Because our faith is in:
        1. "The mighty God"
        2. "The everlasting Father"
        3. "The Prince of Peace"

The Lord our Strength *(Isa. 26:3-4,7)*
   I. There Is Strength in Peace of Mind (v. 3).
  II. There Is Strength in Undaunted Faith (vv. 3b-4a).
 III. There Is Strength in God's Indwelling Presence (v. 4b).
  IV. There Is Strength in the Way of Uprightness (v. 7).

Heaven-Sent Renewal *(Isa. 28:12)*
(Here we find the offer of and the hindrance to revival.)
I. The Need of Spiritual Renewal Assumed
II. The Possibility of Rest and Refreshment Stated
III. The Source of Spiritual Renewal Revealed
IV. The Hope of Spiritual Renewal Rejected

False Security *(Isa. 28:16-17)*
(This text teaches three important lessons.)
I. It Clearly Warns Against Putting Trust in a Refuge of Lies.
II. It Emphasizes the Need of a Sure Foundation for Security.
III. It Reveals That False Security Will Be Obliterated by the Plummet of God's Justice and Judgment.

Hardened Hearts *(Isa. 30:15)*
I. Note the Supreme Offer Stated
  A. Salvation in repentance
  B. Peace, confidence, and strength in spiritual renewal
II. Note the Supreme Source of the Promise
  ("For thus saith the Lord God")
III. Note the Supreme Conclusion Drawn
  ("And ye would not")

The Sin of Ungodly Confidence *(Isa. 31:1-2)*
I. Confidence in Man Power Rather Than God Power Is Disgraceful to God
II. Confidence in the Ease of the World's Support Is Cursed of God
III. Confidence in the Counsel of the Ungodly Brings the Judgment of God
IV. Confidence in the World's Wisdom Rather Than Consulting God Is the Way of Fools

The Example of the Eagle *(Isa. 40:31)*
  I. The Eagle Was Once a Chick Waiting for Growth and Development.
  II. The Eagle's Great Strength Came in Time Through Patient Effort.
  III. The Eagle's Wings Lifted It Through Patient Endurance Above the Pollution and Decay of Earth's Limitations.
  Application—Patience and endurance in Christian service will bring constant renewing of strength.

Living Witnesses *(Isa. 43:12)*
  I. Our Testimony of Salvation Makes Us Living Witnesses for God
  II. Our Separation Unto God from Worldly Idols Makes Us Living Witnesses for God
  III. The Testimony of His Free Grace Upon Us Makes Us Living Witnesses for God

God's Blotter *(Isa. 43:25-26)*
  I. The Blotter Is God's Grace.
  II. The Blotter Thoroughly Removes Every Stain of Our Transgressions.
  III. The Blotter Erases Our Sin from God's Mind.
  IV. The Blotter Assures Our Justification Before God (v. 26).

Spiritual Vision *(Isa. 45:22)*
  I. What? "Look" and See Your Personal Need of Spiritual Aid
  II. Why? "Look" and Find Salvation
  III. Who? "Look Unto Me"
  Application—"I am God, and there is none else."

1. No one else to help
2. No other answer to your need
3. No other way of salvation

Faith and False Light *(Isa. 50:10-11; note three contrasts)*
   I. True Faith as Opposed to False Light
  II. True Vision as Opposed to False Vision
 III. True Conversion as Opposed to False Conversion

Rewards of Returning Backsliders *(Isa. 51:11)*
(Here we have four descriptive phrases expressing the rewards of returning backsliders.)
   I. "Come with Singing."
  II. Everlasting Joy Shall Be Upon Their Head."
 III. "They Shall Obtain Gladness and Joy."
  IV. "Sorrow and Mourning Shall Flee Away."

The Healing Savior *("With his stripes we are healed," Isa. 53:5-6.)*
   I. The Twofold Message
      A. The human race is sick.
      B. Sin needs a remedy.
  II. The Means Revealed
      A. Christ has borne our penalty ("His stripes")
      B. Christ's blood has provided a remedy for us ("We are healed")
 III. The Dangerous Misinformation
      ("We have turned every one to his own way.")
      A. That religion is the answer
      B. That reformation is the answer
      C. That self-righteousness is the answer

The Believer's Husband (*"Thy Maker is thy husband,"* Isa. 54:5.)

I. The Husband Is the Head of the Wife.

II. The Wife Is in Subjection to the Husband.

III. The Husband Is to Be Revered by the Wife.

Application—Emphasize the duties of love we owe to our Lord who claims such a close relationship to us.

Seeking God (*Isa. 55:6-7*)

I. The Two Imperatives
   A. "Seek ye"
   B. "Call ye"

II. The Two Implications
   A. There is a time when God must be approached.
   B. If God is not approached at the right time the door could be closed.

III. The Two Applications
   A. Repentance brings mercy.
   B. Faith brings pardon.

Dual Ministry of God's Word (*Isa. 55:10-11*)

I. It Is Compared with the Effects of Rain and Snow Upon the Earth.
   A. Rain and snow come down from heaven.
   B. They cover the earth with multitudes of blessings.

II. It Is Sent with the Assurance of Accomplishing God's Purpose.
   A. It never returns to God void.
   B. It is prosperous and fruitful wherever it goes.

Stumbling Blocks (*Isa. 57:14*)

I. Stumbling Blocks Prevent a Clear Roadway for Following God's Will.

II. A Prepared Highway to Victory for God's People Comes with Removing of the Stumbling Blocks.

III. God Commands Us to Rebuild the Road of Return to Him. Application—"Take up the stumbling blocks out of the way."

The Great Reviving *(Isa. 57:15)*

I. The Reviving Comes from the High and Holy God.

II. The Reviving Comes in a High and Holy Place.

III. The Reviving Comes Upon High and Holy Conditions.

IV. The Reviving Comes for a High and Holy Purpose.

Great Judgment *(Isa. 59:1-2)*

I. The Great Possibility
("Lord's hand is not shortened," v. 1)

II. The Great Transgression
("Your iniquities . . . your sins," v. 2)

III. The Great Separation
("Your iniquities have separated between you and your God," v. 2)

IV. The Great Rejection
("Hid his face from you that he will not hear," v. 2)

Sure Victory for God's People *(Isa. 59:19-20)*

("The spirit of the Lord shall lift up a standard against him," v. 19*b*)

I. Standard of Heaven Lifted Up

II. Power of Hell Put Down

III. Name of the Lord Glorified

IV. Redeemer of God's People Magnified

God's Doves Flying to His Windows *(Isa. 60:8)*
  I. Indicates That His Chosen People Will Hasten to Their Place of Destination
  II. Indicates a Spirit of Revival in the Regathering
  III. As Clouds Are Driven By the Winds, So God's People Drawn By His Holy Spirit

The God of His People *(Isa. 60:19-20)*
  I. The Lord, the Believer's Everlasting Light
  II. The Lord, the Believer's Glory
  III. The Lord, the Believer's Comfort

Watchman Upon the Walls *(Isa. 62:6,11)*
  I. There as God's Anointed
  II. There to Preach God's Message
  III. There to Intercede for the People Through Prayer
  IV. There as a Reminder That God Fulfills Both Justice and Judgment

Prophecy of Salvation *(Isa. 63:1-6)*
  I. The Great Problem
  II. The Mighty Savior
  III. The Triumph of Calvary
  IV. The Coming Kingdom

The Backslider's Predicament *(Isa. 63:17-19)*
  I. Spiritually Hardened Heart
  II. Sin-Controlled Life
  III. Severed Fellowship with God
  IV. Starving Soul with Guilt Barrier to Renewed Holiness

86

Repulsive Worship *(Isa. 66:1-4)*

(Not all worship in God's name is acceptable to him.)
  I. When It Is Not the Product of a Contrite Heart
  II. When Sin Is in Our Lives
  III. When It Is Token Worship Steeped in Ceremonialism
  IV. When It Is the Product of Man's Doctrine Rather Than Truth

Three Things God Favors in Men *(Isa. 66:2)*
  I. The Humble Man
  II. The Man Who Has a Contrite Heart
  III. The Man with a Fearful Respect for God's Word

Rebirth *(Isa. 66:7-9)*

(Here we have three great truths of the subject outlined)
  I. The Miracle of Rebirth Revealed
  II. The Preordained Plan of Rebirth Stated
  III. The Security by Rebirth Assured

JEREMIAH

The Preacher's Duty *(Jer. 1:10)*
I. To Honor the High Office to Which He Is Called
("Set thee over the nations and over the kingdoms," v. 10*a*)
II. To Take a Stand on Righteous Indignation
("To root out, . . . pull down, . . . destroy, . . . throw down" v. 10*b*)
III. To Be a Wise and Tactful Worker
("To build, and to plant," v. 10*c*)

Reactions of the Natural Heart *(Jer. 2:13)*
I. Natural Heart Inclined to Evil
II. Natural Heart Rejects God, the Fountain of Life-Giving Waters
III. Natural Heart Prefers Leaky Vessels That Constantly Run Dry
IV. Natural Heart Stores Up Worldly Treasures That Last Only for a Short Season

Depravity, Denial, and Deliverance *(Jer. 2:23,28)*
I. The Sinner Does Not Want to See His Sin.
II. The Sinner Must Be Convinced of His Unconverted State.
III. The Sinner Must Be Convinced of God's Displeasure with His Sinful State.
IV. The Sinner Must Turn to God Alone If He Is to Be Delivered from His Sinful State.

Sinners on Difficult Ground *(Jer. 2:25)*
  I. In Love with Freedom to Sin
  II. Willful Rejection of Hope in God
  III. Deceived by Worldly Lusts
  IV. Sold Out to Pleasures of Material Things
  V. Dedicated to Evil Companionship

Self-Deception *(Jer. 2:37)*
  (Note the three ways the text reveals this error.)
  I. By Thinking Happiness in Life Can Come Apart from God
  II. By Thinking True Prosperity Comes Through the Aid of Worldly People
  III. By Thinking Self-Confidence Can Deliver from Acknowledging One's Need of God
  Application—False confidence results in a lifelong headache, "Thy hands upon thine head."

The Sinner's Desperate Hope *(Jer. 3:5)*
  I. That God's Anger Upon Sin Will Be Stayed by His Long-suffering Spirit
  II. That God Will, in the Final Analysis, Excuse His Sin
  III. That He May Persistently Pursue Greater Evil Pleasures with an Attitude of Ease

God's Plea for Sanctification *(Jer. 4:3-4)*
  I. Hardened Hearts Choke Out the Good Seed of Righteousness
  II. God Demands Inward Cleansing Rather Than Outward Ordinances Which Serve Only as an Attempt to Appease One's Conscience
  III. Continued Ungodliness Will Bring the Sure Judgment of God

False Peace *(Jer. 6:14)*

(Four traits of its presence)

I. When It Is Based Upon False Teaching
   (Jeremiah had revealed the error of false prophets of his day)
II. When All Evidence Clearly Points to Unrest and Insecurity
III. When It Is Claimed with a Clear Knowledge That One Has Sin in His Life
IV. When It Is Based Upon Self-Security

Substitutes for True Faith *(Jer. 6:16)*

I. True Faith Is Left Off When We Depart from Walking in "the Old Paths, Where Is the Good Way."
   A. The "old paths" represent the law of God.
   B. The "good way" represents righteousness.
II. True Faith Is Left Off When We Forget That Rest for the Soul Depends Upon Obedience to God.
III. True Faith Is Left Off When We Substitute Our Way for God's Way.

The Unasked Question *("What have I done?" Jer. 8:6.)*

I. It Is a Question the Sinner Avoids.
II. It Is a Question God Wishes the Sinner to Ask Himself.
III. It Is a Question Which, If Avoided Now, the Sinner Will Ask Many Times in Hell.
IV. It Is a Question Which, If Asked Now, May Turn Back the Sinner's Course Wherein He Rushes Farther and Farther from the Possibility of Being Saved.

Weary Sinners *(Delay results in misery, Jer. 13:16.)*

I. The Sinner Seeks Security Where There Is No Assurance.
II. The Sinner Seeks Fulfillment Where There Is Only Guilt.

90

III. The Sinner Seeks a Heavenly Promise with Nothing in
Sight but Perdition.
IV. The Sinner Seeks God's Peace Where There Is Nothing but
the World, Which Supplies Not the Need.
V. The Sinner Seeks to Avoid Death While He Must Arrange
Matters for Dying.

God's Concern for Backsliders ("Woe unto thee, O Jerusalem," Jer. 13:27.)
I. Impenitent Backsliders Have Reason to Expect Woe.
II. God Has No Pleasure in Inflicting Woe Upon His People.
III. The Apostasy and Unfaithfulness of Backsliders Can Lead
Them to Imagine They Have No Need for Cleansing.
IV. God Seeks to Stir the Conscience of Backsliders so That
They May Repent ("Wilt thou not be made clean?")

The Judgment (Jer. 17:10)
I. God's Searching Tribunal
II. Man's Inescapable Accounting
III. The Fair and Just Judgment
IV. The Strict Rules Applied
  A. No appeals
  B. No reprieves
  C. No revision of judgment
  D. No stay of execution
  E. No paroles

Divine Change Necessary (Jer. 18:1-6)
I. "Marred" Clay Is a Perfect Description of Human Nature.
II. The Renewed "Pot" Is a Perfect Description of the Divine
Change Necessary.

III. The "Potter" Is a Perfect Description of the Divine Agency by Which the Change Is Brought About.
IV. The "Wheels" Are a Perfect Description of the Means God Has Given by Which the Divine Change Is Accomplished.

God's Power Over His People *(Jer. 18:6)*
I. Primary Application Was to Israel
II. The Application Can Be Made to the Church
   A. As individual members
   B. As a collective body
   C. As to the effect the application should have on us
III. The Expectancy with Which We Should Submit Ourselves to That Power

The Burning Word *("But his Word was in mine heart as a burning fire," Jer. 20:9.)*
I. The Word Burns to Make Us Submissive Witnesses for God
II. The Word Burns to Remind Us of the Fate of Sinners If We Forbear to Witness
III. The Word Burns to Call Us to Service Which, If We Stay, Adds Misery to Our Lives ("Fire shut up in my bones").

Reasonable Response to God *(Jer. 21:8)*
I. God Offers the Way of Life.
   A. Physical life is in the gift of natural birth.
   B. Spiritual life comes only through the new birth.
II. God Warns of the Way of Death.
   A. Natural death is a part of living.
   B. Spiritual death is man's judgment for the sin of unbelief.

III. Man's Option Is to Choose Either the Way of Life or the Way of Death.
   A. The reasonable response would be to choose the way of life in spite of natural birth.
   B. The unreasonable response is to choose spiritual death by rejecting the way of eternal life.

Israel and Judah's Example to Sinners *(Jer. 50:4-5)*
   I. Sorrowful Repentance
      ("Going and Weeping")
   II. Earnestly Seeking
      ("And seek the Lord their God")
   III. Faithfully Trusting God to Lead Them Home
      ("They shall ask the way to Zion with their faces thitherward.")
   IV. Vowing Perpetual Service to God
      ("Let us join ourselves to the Lord in a perpetual covenant that shall not be forgotten.")

LAMENTATIONS

The Backslider's Lament *(Lam. 1:1-2)*
(Jerusalem's plight can be taken as representative of the backslider's sorrows.)
  I. The Backslider Is Lonely.
 II. The Backslider Lives with Grief.
III. The Backslider Is a Slave to Human Nature.
 IV. The Backslider Has Cut Himself Off from the Fellowship of the Righteous.
  V. The Backslider Has Brought Reproach upon Himself.

The Backslider's Humiliation *(Lam. 1:7-12)*
(Jerusalem's plight can be taken as representative of the backslider's humiliation)
  I. Memory of Precious Joys Struck Down By the Enemy (v. 7)
 II. Dishonored by Former Friends (v. 8)
III. Lies in the Gutter of Sin with No Human Way Out (v. 9)
 IV. Subjected to the Will of the Enemy (v. 10)
  V. Suffering the Humiliation of God's Chastisement Before the Enemy (vv. 11-12)

The Soul's Search *(Lam. 3:24-26)*

I. The Soul's Desire

("The Lord is my portion, saith my soul," v. 24*a*)

II. The Soul's Expectancy

("Therefore will I hope in him," v. 24*b*.)

III. The Soul's Patience

("The Lord is good unto them that wait for him, to the soul that seeketh him," v. 25)

IV. The Soul's Search Ended

("It is good that a man should . . . wait for the salvation of the Lord," v. 26.)

EZEKIEL

The Preacher's Hard Duty *(Ezek. 2:7-8)*

I. The Preacher Must Preach God's Message in Hard Circumstances.

II. The Preacher Must Preach God's Message to Hardened Hearts.

III. The Preacher Must Preach God's Message When He Is Tempted to Rebel.

IV. The Preacher Must Preach God's Message Because It Is Given to Him from God.

Warning to the Wicked *(Ezek. 3:17-19)*

I. God Has Provided a Message to Warn the Wicked of the Consequence of Continuing in Sin (v. 17).

II. God Emphasizes the Grave Responsibility Placed upon the Messenger as Regards the Mission Entrusted to Him (v. 18).

III. God Clearly Shows the Personal Responsibility of the Wicked to Hear and Deliver His Soul (v. 19).

Sin and Judgment *(Ezek. 5:5-17)*

I. A Sinful, Backslidden People (vv. 5-7)

II. A Shocking Prediction (vv. 8-15)

III. A Sorrowing Message Preached (vv. 16-17)
Note—God always warns before sending judgment.

The Trial of Faith *(Ezek. 9:3-6)*

I. Faith Protects God's People

    A. The man with the inkhorn (v. 3)

B. Set a mark on the foreheads (v. 4)

C. Go through the city and smite (v. 5)

II. Do You Really Believe?

A. Any man upon whom the mark (v. 6)

B. And begin at my sanctuary (v. 6)

C. How would your profession stand up under such scrutiny?

Story of Redemption in Ezekiel's Prophecy *(Ezek. 16:1-14)*

I. Sinners By Nature (v. 3)

II. Sinner's Former Destitution (v. 5)

III. Sinner Shown God's Favor (v. 6)

IV. Sinner Blessed with Great Salvation (vv. 8-9)

V. Sinner's New Standing Before God (vv. 10-14)

Saints in the Hands of Satan *(Ezek. 16:54)*

(When can such a state exist?)

I. When We Bear the Shame of Willful, Open Sin

II. When We Are Confounded By Personal Sin Before Sinners

III. When Our Sin and Punishment Is a Comfort to Sinners

Perdition *(Ezek. 18:32)*

This text clearly shows

I. That Perdition Is a Displeasure to God

II. That Perdition Is a Moral Issue Subject to the Will of Man

III. That Perdition Does Not Have to Be the Lot of Man as He Is Given a Choice in the Matter

Amusement in Sin *("Should we then make mirth?" Ezek. 21:10.)*
   I. It Is Warned Against (see Gal. 6:7).
   II. It Is Foolish in Time of Danger.
   III. It Is Blinding as Regards the Judgment It Brings.

A Day of Reckoning *(Ezek. 22:14)*
   I. It Will Be Intolerable.
   II. It Will Be Unavoidable.
   III. It Is Appointed by the Word of God.

The Neglected Warning *(Ezek. 33:5)*
   I. Sinners Are Neglecting God's Warning in Time of Great Peril.
   II. Sinners Are Neglecting the Sound of the Trumpet (means by which God sounds forth his message).
   III. Sinners Continue to Neglect Though the Doom Be Already Pronounced.

Complete Renewal *(Ezek. 36:26-27)*
   I. The Problem—a "Stony Heart"
   II. The Promise
      A. "A new heart"
      B. "A new spirit"
   III. The Provider—God ("I Will")
   IV. The Principle ("I will . . . cause you to walk in my statutes," v. 27.)

DANIEL

Daniel the Conqueror *(Dan. 1:18)*

I. He Conquered the Temptation of Youthful Desires Toward Ungodliness.

II. He Conquered the Temptation to Please Men Rather Than God.

III. He Conquered the Temptation to Forsake the Faith of His Fathers.

Conclusion—The faithfulness of Daniel in a brief moment of his life brought great blessings from God.

1. He raised Daniel up as a young nobleman before the state officials.

2. He raised Daniel up as a great statesman in a foreign land.

3. He raised Daniel up as a superb prophet.

Rewards for Faith *("There is a God in heaven," Dan. 2:28.)*

I. God Rewarded Daniel's Faith by Revealing the Meaning of the King's Dreams and Visions.

II. God Rewarded Daniel's Faith by Delivering Him from the Lion's Den.

III. God Rewarded Daniel's Faith by Revealing to Him the Future of His People, Israel.

Tekel *(Dan. 5:27)*

Note three things regarding sinners:

I. They Are Weighed in the Balance of God's Moral Law.

II. They Are Tried and Found Defective.

III. Their Judgment Is Already Written.

Daniel's Bravery *(Dan. 6:10,16,22)*
I. Bravery in Spite of an Evil Plot Against Him (v. 10)
II. Bravery in Prayer Though It Put His Life on the Line
(v. 10)
III. Bravery in the Lion's Den (vv. 16,22)
Application—Dare to be a Daniel.

The God Who Is Able to Deliver *(Dan. 6:20-22)*
I. Consider Some Gods That Cannot Deliver.
A. The god of wealth
1. Proved by the fate of rich young ruler (Luke 12)
2. Proved by the rich man in hell (Luke 16)
B. The god of false religion ("The truth shall make you
free," John 8:32.)
C. The god of atheism (Ps. 53:1)
II. Daniel Served the True God Who Could Deliver
A. His test of faith (v. 20)
B. His testimony of faith (vv. 21-22)
III. Daniel's Accusers Had No Source of Deliverance (v. 24).

Daniel's Supplication *(Dan. 9:18)*
I. It Was a Prayer of Repentance in Behalf of His People.
II. It Was a Prayer Which Rejected a Self-Righteous Attitude.
III. It Was a Prayer Offered Totally upon the Merit of God's
Mercy.

HOSEA

Spiritual Reunion (*"I will go and return to my first husband; for then it was better with me than now," Hos. 2:7.*)
I. The Text Implies the Resolving of a Former Union with God.
II. The Text Implies That the Union Was Resolved By Man's Unfaithfulness to God.
III. The Text Implies That the Innate Being of Man Desires a Spiritual Reunion with God.
IV. The Text Implies That the Initiative of the Reuniting Rests upon Man Who Broke the Union.

Escape from the Valley of Troubles (*Hos. 2:15*)
I. God Can Transform Our Valley of Trouble into a Path of Encouragement.
II. God Can Give Blessings Which Far Surpass All We May Have Counted Loss.
III. God Can Bear Our Troubles with Us and Bring Rejoicing to Us.
IV. God Can, By Reminding Us of Past Blessings, Open the Door of New Hope.

Controversy (*Hos. 4:1-4*)
Here we have:
I. The Lord's Controversy with His People (v. 1)
II. The Cause of the Controversy (v. 2)
III. The Result of That Controversy (v. 3)
IV. A Directive Concerning That Controversy (v. 4)
Note—Verse 4 is actually saying, "Don't pass the buck, accept your personal responsibility for guilt."

Spiritual Ignorance Among God's People *(Hos. 4:6)*
I. Its Basis Is a Willful Ignorance of God's Word.
("Seeing thou hast forgotten the law of thy God.")
II. It Leads to a Backslidden Condition.
("My people are destroyed [cut off spiritually] for the lack of knowledge.")
III. It Results in the Withdrawal of God's Fellowship.
("Because thou hast rejected knowledge, I will also reject thee.")

Backsliders Healed and Revived *(Hos. 6:1-2)*
I. It Is the Lord Who Chastises His Disobedient People (v. 1).
("He hath torn, . . . he hath smitten")
II. It Is the Lord Who Restores His People to His Favor When They Repent and Turn Back to Him (v. 1).
III. It Is the Lord Who Sends Revival into the Hearts of His Penitent People (v. 2).

Gilgal—The Good and the Bad *("All their wickedness is in Gilgal," Hos. 9:15.)*
I. The Good
A. Gilgal was where the Israelites set up the twelve stones commemorating their crossing of Jordan.
B. Gilgal was where the Israelites observed the circumcision of sanctification unto the Lord.
C. Gilgal was where the Israelites observed the Passover in the new land.
D. Gilgal was where the Lord appeared to Joshua as the captain of heaven's hosts.
II. The Bad
A. Gilgal was a city where Baal worship flourished.

B. Gilgal was where the monarchy, despised of God, was instituted (1 Sam. 11:15).

Conclusion—"There I hated them."

Spiritual Farming By Seeking God—*(Hos. 10:12)*
I. The Preparation
  A. Breaking up the hardened ground of the heart
  B. Sowing unto ourselves in righteousness
  C. Seeking the Lord "till he come"
II. The Prospects
  A. We will reap a crop of mercy.
  B. God will rain his righteousness upon us.
  C. The blessings conferred upon us will be our assurance of salvation.

God's Lament for Backsliders *(Hos. 11:8-9)*
I. Behold God's Claim Upon His People
II. Behold God's Searching Concern for His Backslidden Children
III. Behold God's Inward Hurt Over His Backslidden Children (They break his heart)
IV. Behold God's Long-Suffering Mercy Upon His Backslidden Children (v. 9)

The Great Curse and the Great Help *(Hos. 13:9)*
I. The Curse
  ("O Israel, thou hast destroyed thyself")
  A. As Israel was cursed, so is the sinner
  B. As Israel's curse was self-inflicted, so is the sinner's
II. The Help
  ("But in me is thine help")
  A. Israel had only one way to turn—to God.
  B. The sinner has but one way to turn—to Christ (John 14:6).

JOEL

Lament for a Fruitless Harvest *(Joel 1:8-13)*
    I. The Evil of Sin Is Impressed Upon Us by It.
   II. A Renewal of Dependence Upon God Is Inspired by It.
  III. Our Sense of Religious Duty Is Improved by It.

Seven Steps Back to God *(Joel 2:12-20)*
      I. The Sorrowing People (vv. 12-13)
     II. The Sinning Forsaken (v. 14)
   III. The Sanctifying Call (vv. 15-16)
  IV. The Supplication Offered (v. 17)
    V. The Satisfaction Acknowledged (vv. 18-19)
  VI. The Separation Announced (v. 20)
VII. The Salvation Promised (v. 20)

AMOS

Affinity *(Amos 3:3)*
  I. It Calls for Agreement with God.
  II. It Calls for Unity Among Christians.
  III. It Calls for Cooperation Within the Body of Christ.

"Prepare to Meet Thy God" *(Amos 4:12)*
  I. "Thy God"
  (He will be everyone's personal God, either in salvation or in judgment.)
  II. "Meet"
  (Everyone will have to face him to give a personal account.)
  III. "Prepare"
  (All are called to make sure of their personal readiness.)

Seek and Live *(Amos 5:6)*
  I. The Urging Employed
  ("Seek the Lord.")
  II. The Promise Given
  ("And ye shall live")
  III. The Judgment Warning
  ("Lest he break out like fire . . . and there be none to quench it.")

No Escape for Evil Men *(Amos 5:19-20)*
  Some things the text reveals:
  I. That Evil Is Ever Present with Evil Men
  II. That Evil Men Who Seek to Flee from One Evil Always Meet with Another

III. That the Evils of Men Will Betray Them in the Day of God's Light

The Lord Is His Name *(Amos 6:8)*
   I. The Injunction
      "Seek him."
   II. The Revelation
      A. He is all-knowing.
      B. He is all-powerful.
      C. He is everywhere present.
   III. The Application
      A. Fear him.
      B. Seize upon his mercy.
      C. Seek his forgiveness.

Means of Revival *(Amos 7:1-3)*
   I. A Vision of Judgment Upon a Disobedient People (v. 1)
   II. An Intercessory Prayer for God's Mercy Upon His People (v. 2)
   III. God Relents and Spares His People from Judgment
      Application—Just the thought of what God could do but refuses to do because of his love for us ought to create a desire for revival.

OBADIAH

Tragedy of a Prideful Heart *(Obad. 3)*

    I. Pride Deceives Us in Regard to Our Dependence Upon God.

    II. Pride Deceives Us in Regard to False Security.

    III. Pride Deceives Us in Regard to God's Purpose and Power.

    IV. Pride Deceives Us in Regard to the Destruction Secured by Our Evil Ways.

JONAH

The Disobedient Prophet *(Jonah 1:1-3)*
    I. The Call (v. 1)
    II. The Commission (v. 2)
    III. The Cowardice (v. 3)

Lament of the Disobedient *(Jonah 1:12)*
    I. The Lament of Self-Condemnation
    II. The Lament of Self-Destruction
    III. The Lament of Involving the Innocent Through Self-indulgence
    IV. The Lament of Despair Through the Necessity of Self-Sacrifice

Divine Protection *(Jonah 1:17)*
    I. God Prepared a Life Raft for His Servant on the Sea of Self-Will.
    II. God Never Forsakes His Anointed Servants, Though They May Forsake Him.
    III. God Gives the Disobedient Servant Ample Time to Repent

A Prayer from the Belly of Hell *(Jonah 2:1-10)*
    I. Jonah Was Fully Awakened to His Sin Against God.
    II. Jonah Confessed His Guilt and Accepted the Full Responsibility for His Plight.
    III. Jonah Was in Great Trouble and Despair, but Not Without Hope.
    IV. Jonah, Hopeless of Saving Himself, Fully Trusted in God to Answer His Prayer from the Belly of Hell.

Repentance, Faith, and Salvation *(Jonah 3:5-10)*
  I. The Repentance (vv. 6-8)
  II. The Faith (vv. 5,9)
  III. The Salvation (v. 10)

The Burden of Jonah
  I. Consider the Burden God Placed Upon Jonah (1:1-3).
  II. Consider the Power of God to Use a Person Who Will Submit to His Will (3:1-10).
  III. Consider the Burden with Which Jonah Accepted God's Victory (4:1-11).

MICAH

God's Injunction Against Worldliness *(Mic. 2:10)*
  I. The Command to Arise and Depart from Worldliness
  II. The Reasons Given for Departing from the World
  A. "It is not your rest."
  B. "It is polluted."
  III. The Danger Involved in Neglecting the Command
  ("It shall destroy you, even with a sore destruction.")

The Great Emancipator *(Mic. 2:13)*
  I. As the Breaker, Jesus Has Gone Before Us, Breaking the Power of Sin's Curse.
  II. As the Breaker, Jesus Has Gone Before Us, Breaking the Power of Satan Over Us.
  III. As the Breaker, Jesus Has Gone Before Us, Conquering the Power of the World for Us.
  IV. As the Breaker, Jesus Has Gone Before Us, Opening a Door to Heaven for Us.

Faith in Time of Persecution *(Mic. 7:5-7)*
  I. True Faith Avoids Misguided Confidence (v. 5).
  II. True Faith Looks to God for Guidance (v. 7a).
  III. True Faith Patiently Waits for God's Guidance (v. 7b).
  IV. True Faith Dutifully Prays Until God's Guidance Arrives (v. 7c).

The Character of God *(Mic. 7:18)*

I. The Character of God Distinguishes Him from the Gods of Idolatrous Nations.

("Who . . . is like unto thee?")

II. The Character of God Is to Pardon the Penitent.

III. The Character of God Delights in Mercy.

NAHUM

Judgment and Justice In God's Moral Government
(Nah. 1:2-3)
I. God's Jealousy Assures Us of His Justice.
   A. He is jealous over those he loves.
   B. He takes vengeance upon those who oppress them.
II. God's Revenge Assures Us of His Judgment.
   A. Sin will not go unpunished.
   B. Sinners cannot resist the judgment of God.

God's Revelation to His Saints *(Nah. 1:7)*
I. The Character of His Holiness
   ("The Lord is good.")
II. The Assurance of His Help
   ("A strong hold in the day of trouble.")
III. The Knowledge He Holds
   ("He knoweth them that trust in him.")

HABAKKUK

Persistent Prayer *(Hab. 1:2)*

I. Preachers Must Sometimes Pray and Wait Long for an Answer.

II. Churches and Christians Must Sometimes Pray and Wait Long for an Answer.

III. Salvation of Sinners Often Comes Only After Long, Persistent Praying.

IV. Genuine Revival Often Comes Only After Long, Persistent Praying.

God Among His Worshiping Saints *(Hab. 2:20)*

I. God Honors His Gathered Saints with His Presence

II. Assembly of the Church for Worship Is a Command (Heb. 10:25)

III. God Seeks to Manifest Himself to His People by Drawing Them Together for Their Adoration, Prayers, and Communication

Habakkuk's Prayer *(Hab. 3:1-2)*

I. It Was a Devout Prayer.

II. It Was a Prayer Seeking Genuine Revival.

III. It Was a Prayer Seeking Divine Mercy in the Face of Possible Calamity.

IV. It Was a Prayer Made in Recognition of the Necessity of Spiritual Renewal by the Intervening Hand of God.

ZEPHANIAH

Atheistic Deception *(Zeph. 1:12)*

Here we have:
  I. The Practice of Atheism
   A. Open denial of the agency of divine providence
   B. Indifference toward moral integrity as produced by such practice
  II. The Pronounced Judgment of God Upon Atheism
   A. The light of God exposes their foolish philosophy
   B. Punishment of God is revealed as a principal law recorded by his own hand
  III. The Personal Deception of Atheism
   A. Belief that man is answerable to self alone
   B. Belief that there is no divine light to expose immorality

Disobedience, the Road of Backsliders *(Zeph. 3:1-7)*

(Judah's spiritual decline teaches a modern lesson for backsliders.)
  I. Description of Backslidden Judah (v. 1)
   "Filthy and polluted"
  II. Rebellion of Backslidden Judah (v. 2)
   A. Ignored the voice of God
   B. Rejected God's efforts toward her correction
   C. Forsook her faith in God
   D. Abandonment of God
  III. Degradation of Backslidden Judah (vv. 3-4)
   A. Political pollution (v. 3)
   B. Religious pollution (v. 4)
  IV. Judgment of Backslidden Judah (vv. 5-7)
   Application—Backsliders have two choices:
   1. Continual rebellion and judgment
   2. Repentance and forgiveness

Three Divine Principles Revealed Through Historical Disasters *(Zeph. 3:6-8)*

I. Divine Calamities Permitted (v. 6)

II. Moral Improvement Motivated (v. 7)

III. Retribution Designed for the Disobedient (v. 8)

HAGGAI

Dereliction of Religious Duty *(Hag. 1:2-8)*
  I. Procrastination
     A. They were putting personal welfare before duty to God.
     B. They were seeking personal security while ignoring spiritual needs.
  II. Provocation
     A. The result was a withholding of God's blessings.
     B. Personal efforts to gain were like earning wages "to put into a bag with holes."
  III. Proclamation
     A. Put first things first.
     B. God will be glorified and his people blessed.

Spiritual Blessings *(Hag. 2:9)*
  I. The Foundation of the Spiritual House Is the Beginning of Divine Blessings.
  II. In the Spiritual Relationship to God Lies the Only True Source of Peace.
  III. We Receive Increasing Blessings from the Day the Foundation of the Spiritual House Is Laid.

116

ZECHARIAH

Little Things *(Zech. 4:10)*
  I. Where Would We Be Without Little Things?
    A. Seeds for growing food
    B. Sparks for source of heat, electricity, etc.
    C. Mountain streams to provide large bodies of water
    D. Children to carry on the race
  II. Jesus Emphasized the Importance of Little Things in Relation to the Spiritual Realm.
    A. Lilies of the field
    B. The sparrows
    C. The widow's mite
    D. The lad's loaves and fishes
    E. Called little children unto him
    F. Uneducated fishermen
    G. Twelve disciples (nucleus of great church)

Sin Sickness and a Cure *(Zech. 8:13)*
  I. The Former Curse
  II. The Possibility of Salvation
  III. The Promised Blessing
    Note—A curse was changed to a blessing because of God's grace unto salvation.

MALACHI

Dishonoring God *(Mal. 1:6-8)*
  I. God Gives an Example of Customary Honor (v. 6).
   A. Human son's honor for his father
   B. Human servant's fearful honor for his master
 II. God Seeks to Draw a Conclusion from That Example (v. 6).
   A. How much more honor is deserved by your Heavenly Father!
   B. How much more holy fear is deserved by your Heavenly Master!
III. God Rejects Hypocritical Servitude (vv. 7-8).
   A. He points out their open dishonor in worship by offering polluted sacrifices to him
   B. He points out their lack of fear in offering to him that which even their human governor would reject
Conclusion—Our failure to discharge honorable service to God cannot be compensated for by moral integrity in relation to our fellowman.

The Coming Kingdom *(Mal. 1:11)*
   "Thy kingdom come" (Matt. 6:10)
  I. Its Universal Scope
   A. All people of the earth
   B. Every place upon earth
 II. Its Universal Diffusion
   A. Adoration of God's character
   B. Common worship of pure religion
III. Its Universal Perfection
   A. Emulation of God's character
   B. Manifestation of perfect harmony

118